Welcome to God's Family

A Foundational Guide for Spirit-Filled Living

Welcome to God's Family

A Foundational Guide for Spirit-Filled Living

Kenneth E. Hagin

Unless otherwise indicated, all Scripture quotations are taken from the *King James Version* of the Bible.

22 21 20 19 18 17 16   14 13 12 11 10 09 08

Welcome to God's Family
ISBN-13: 978-0-89276-528-7
ISBN-10: 0-89276-528-3

In the U.S. write:
Kenneth Hagin Ministries
P.O. Box 50126
Tulsa, OK 74150-0126
1-888-28-FAITH
rhema.org

In Canada write:
Kenneth Hagin Ministries of Canada
P.O. Box 335, Station D
Etobicoke (Toronto), Ontario
Canada M9A 4X3
1-866-70-RHEMA
rhemacanada.org

Kenneth Hagin Ministries gratefully acknowledges the permission of Kenyon's Gospel Publishing Society, Lynnwood, WA, to include the author's paraphrases and quotations of portions of *Sign Posts on the Road to Success* by E.W. Kenyon.

Contents

Preface

As a member of God's family, you have a responsibility to grow and be fruitful in your Christian walk. Compiled in this book are several of my best-selling minibooks that deal with the basics of foundational Christian living. They have been reedited and reformatted to help you become rooted and *remain* rooted and grounded in the eternal truths of God's Word.

Just as a person in the natural must receive physical nourishment to grow, develop, and be sustained properly, Christians must constantly receive spiritual nourishment in order to grow and develop spiritually as God intends. The content of this book is devoted to both the new believer and the more mature believer in Christ to use as food for meditation and practice. When applied, the truths contained in this book will greatly assist the believer in *"Holding fast the faithful word as he hath been taught, that he may be able by sound doctrine both to exhort and to convince . . ."* (Titus 1:9).

The truth of God's Word never grows old! I encourage you to constantly meditate along the lines of who you are in Christ and what you have received as a new creation in Him and a member of God's family. The apostle Peter said, *"For if these things be in you, and abound, they make you that ye shall neither be barren nor unfruitful in the knowledge of our Lord Jesus Christ"* (2 Peter 1:8). My prayer is that you may produce fruit that remains and that in walking with God and serving Him, your joy may be made full (John 15:11, 16).

—Kenneth E. Hagin

— Chapter 1 —
Understanding the New Birth

"It's not important what church you are in. The important thing is: What *family* are you in?"

Therefore if any man be in Christ, he is a new creature [creation]: old things are passed away, behold, all things are become new.
—2 Corinthians 5:17

The key which unlocks all the promises of God can be found in becoming a child of God. Jesus taught that a man must be born again. The following statements came from the lips of Jesus:

"*. . . Except a man be born again, he cannot see the kingdom of God*" (John 3:3).

"*. . . Except a man be born of water and of the Spirit, he cannot enter into the kingdom of God*" (John 3:5).

"*. . . Except ye be converted, and become as little children, ye shall not enter into the kingdom of heaven*" (Matt. 18:3).

1

". . . Except ye repent, ye shall all likewise perish" (Luke 13:3, 5).

The New Birth is a necessity to being saved. Through the New Birth, you come into right relationship with God. The New Birth is necessary before you can claim any of the benefits of the Bible.

The New Birth is *not*: confirmation; church membership; water baptism; the taking of sacraments; observing religious duties; an intellectual reception of Christianity; orthodoxy of faith; going to church; saying prayers; reading the Bible; being moral; being cultured or refined; doing good deeds; doing your best or doing any of the many other things in which some people are trusting to save them.

Nicodemus, whom Jesus addressed concerning the New Birth, possessed most of the qualities we just listed, but Jesus said to him, *". . . Ye must be born again"* (John 3:7).

The thief on the cross and others whom Jesus forgave while on earth were saved without these things. They simply did the one necessary thing: They accepted Jesus Christ as their personal Savior by repenting and turning to God with their whole heart, as a little child.

One who is born again will automatically have the external evidences of a good life by virtue of the

New Birth. But there are millions, it is sad to say, who are trusting in good works to save them. And millions will die and be lost without the New Birth, because they have been misled concerning the experience of being born again.

It is all important that we pay personal attention to our eternal welfare and that we not trust the best of men in the matter. If we permit men to mislead us in eternal matters and are lost, it will be too late to personally see after our welfare. Do something about it now.

Don't take the attitude that you cannot be deceived. Don't take the attitude that your church is the only right one and that it cannot mislead you. Your church may be right in its teaching concerning the New Birth. But make certain by going to the Bible yourself, seeing with your own eyes and knowing with your own heart that you are right with God—that you have the real New Birth—and that you are living right with God every day.

There is no purpose served in fooling yourself. You are either born again or you are not. You are either really saved or you are being deceived into thinking you are, and you are lost.

You know your own life and your true relationship to God. So get the facts settled that you are a genuinely saved person and in present contact with God.

Culture, refinements, and outward correctness of life—in the organized church or out of it—cannot take the place of the New Birth. For the trouble, you see, is in the heart.

Jesus said, *"For from within, out of the heart of men, proceed evil thoughts, adulteries, fornications, murders, Thefts, covetousness, wickedness, deceit, lasciviousness, an evil eye, blasphemy, pride, foolishness: All these evil things come from within, and defile the man"* (Mark 7:21–23).

The trouble is in the heart, the inward man, the spirit. To merely reform the outward man or the outward life will not save you.

An artist could put a beautifully colored coating of wax on the outside of a rotten apple—but the apple would still be rotten at heart. One bite into it would be a bite into decay.

Outside of Christ, every man is rotten in the heart. And mere outward correctness of life, apart from Christ, is artificial and the practice of hypocrites. Jesus said to those He called hypocrites: *". . . ye are like unto whited sepulchres, which indeed*

4

appear beautiful outward, but are within full of dead men's bones, and of all uncleanness" (Matt. 23:27).

From Death Unto Life

The Bible is a mystery book until we find the key that opens it. Then it ceases to be a mystery and becomes a message. There are two words which open up the Bible to our understanding—and those words are *life* and *death*.

Death has been a mystery in all ages. Science stands utterly mute in its presence, unable to explain it. Philosophy turns poetical when it meets this dread enemy of man. And theology has dealt only in generalities when attempting to explain it.

Death, that bloodhound-like foe, began its work at the cradle of the human race and has followed the human race down through the stream of the centuries until the present hour. Death was not a part of the Creation, nor a part of God's original plan. Even physical death is an enemy of God and an enemy of man. The Bible says in First Corinthians 15:26 that physical death is the last enemy that shall be put underfoot.

Before we can understand the nature of death, however, we must understand the nature of man. Man is not a physical being. Man is a spirit. In fact, man *is* a *spirit* who *possesses* a *soul* and *lives in* a *body* (1 Thess. 5:23).

When Jesus told Nicodemus, *". . . Ye must be born again"* (John 3:7), Nicodemus was thinking naturally, and he asked, *". . . How can a man be born when he is old? can he enter the second time into his mother's womb, and be born?"* (John 3:4). And Jesus explained, *"That which is born of the flesh is flesh; and that which is born of the Spirit is spirit"* (John 3:6).

The New Birth is the rebirth of the human spirit!

The real man is spirit. The spirit operates through the soul (man's intellect, emotions, and will). And the soul in turn operates through the physical body.

Now the man, who is spirit, and his soul live in a physical body. At physical death, the man and his soul leave the physical body and go to their eternal home.

Christ gave us Luke 16:19–24, the experience of the rich man and Lazarus.

LUKE 16:19–24
19 There was a certain rich man, which was clothed in purple and fine linen, and fared sumptuously every day:
20 And there was a certain beggar named Lazarus, which was laid at his gate, full of sores,
21 And desiring to be fed with the crumbs which fell from the rich man's table: moreover the dogs came and licked his sores.

22 And it came to pass, that the beggar died, and was carried by the angels into Abraham's bosom: the rich man also died, and was buried;

23 And in hell he lift up his eyes, being in torments, and seeth Abraham afar off, and Lazarus in his bosom.

24 And he cried and said, Father Abraham, have mercy on me, and send Lazarus, that he may dip the tip of his finger in water, and cool my tongue; for I am tormented in this flame.

Lazarus and the rich man were still conscious. Man is not dead like an animal as some folks would have you believe. And there is no such thing as "soul sleep."

Several kinds of deaths are spoken of in the Bible, but there are three kinds with which we need to familiarize ourselves: 1) spiritual death; 2) physical death; and 3) eternal death or the Second Death, which is being cast into the lake which burneth with fire and brimstone (Rev. 21:8).

Spiritual death came to the earth first, then manifested itself in the physical body by destroying it. Physical death is but a manifestation of the law which is at work within, called by Paul, *". . . the law of sin and death"* (Rom. 8:2).

When God said to Adam, *". . . in the day that thou eatest thereof thou shalt surely die"* (Gen. 2:17), He did not refer to physical death but to spiritual death.

7

If man had never died spiritually, he would not have died physically.

Spiritual Death Means
Separation From God

The moment Adam sinned, he was separated from God. And when God came down in the cool of the day, as was His custom, to walk and talk with Adam, God called out, "Adam, where art thou?" Adam said, "I hid myself" (Gen. 3:9–10). He was separated from God.

Man was now united with the devil. He is an outcast, an outlaw, driven from the Garden with no legal ground of approach to God. He no longer responds to the call of God. He responds only to his new nature or to his new master. Man is more than a transgressor. He is more than a lawbreaker and a sinner. Man is spiritually a child of the devil, and he partakes of his father's nature.

This explains why man cannot be saved by conduct. He has to be born again. If man were not a child of the devil, then he could just begin to "put on" the right kind of conduct, and he'd be all right. But even if he puts on right conduct, he's still a child of the devil and will go to hell when he dies—to the lake which burneth with fire and brimstone, which is the Second Death (Rev. 21:8).

Man cannot stand in the Presence of God as he is, because he has the nature of his father, the devil, in him. If man is ever saved, he has to be saved by Someone paying the penalty for his sins and by Someone giving him a new nature.

You might take a flop-eared mule and try to make a racehorse of him. You could file his teeth and polish his hooves. You could feed him the finest food, run him around the track every day, and house him in the finest stable. But on the day of the race when the gun sounds, all he'll do is lope off down the track—because he's a mule! Being a racehorse is just not in him.

Yet you could take a racehorse and not give him as much care, but when you put him on the starting line and the gun sounds—he's off! It's his nature to race. He's born and bred that way. But in order for that old mule to be a racehorse, he would have to be reborn— and that's impossible.

Man, however, who is a spirit, living in a body, can be reborn. His nature can be changed. He can become a new creature in Christ Jesus!

It doesn't matter how well-educated a man becomes, how many degrees he has at the end of his name, how many dollars he has, how good a social worker he is, or how religious he is—man on his own cannot stand in the Presence of God. His nature is wrong. Man is lost today, not because of what he does, but because of what he *is*. (What he does is the result of what he is.) Man needs life from God, because man is spiritually dead.

Thanks be to God, Christ has redeemed us from spiritual death!

> **JOHN 5:26**
> **26 For as the Father hath life in himself; so hath he given to the Son to have life in himself.**

The new Man, Jesus Christ, had no death in Him. He was not conceived as we are conceived, and He didn't have the spiritual nature of death—the devil— in Him. Yet the Bible says in Hebrews 2:9 that He tasted death for every man.

Jesus Christ took upon Himself our sin nature. Hebrews 9:26 says He *". . . put away SIN* [not sins] *by the sacrifice of himself."* He took upon Himself our sin nature, the nature of spiritual death, that we might have eternal life.

Jesus said, *"The thief* [the devil] *cometh not, but for to steal, and to kill, and to destroy: I am come that they might have life, and that they might have it more abundantly"* (John 10:10).

He also said, *". . . I say unto you, He that heareth my word, and believeth on him that sent me, hath everlasting life, and shall not come into condemnation; but is passed from death unto life"* (John 5:24).

Jesus came to redeem us from spiritual death! Adam was banished from the Tree of Life through rejecting God's Word. According to Revelation 2:7, all who now accept and obey the Word of God are brought back to the Tree of Life.

The New Birth does not take place gradually. It is instantaneous! It is a gift of God received the moment we believe.

In Ephesians 2:1 it says that you who were dead in trespasses and sins—spiritual death—He has quickened, made alive. And verses 8 and 9 tell you how it came about:

EPHESIANS 2:8–9
8 For by grace are ye saved through faith; and that not of yourselves: it is the gift of God:
9 Not of works, lest any man should boast.

"Not of works." That punctures the balloon of the ego. Man wants to *do* something to save himself. He wants to have a part in it. But he can't.

You have to simply admit your helplessness and your hopelessness. You have to admit that you are just what the Bible says you are—a lost sinner. Then you can come and accept what Christ has wrought for you—a gift!

11

Have you passed from spiritual death unto spiritual life? Is God your Father? Can you look up to Heaven and say, "Father, God"? Is His Spirit within your spirit bearing witness that you are a child of God? Do you have the Holy Spirit in your spirit, crying, "Abba, Father"?

You do if you are born again.

> **ROMANS 8:14–16**
> **14 For as many as are led by the Spirit of God, they are the sons of God.**
> **15 For ye have not received the spirit of bondage again to fear; but ye have received the Spirit of adoption, whereby we cry, Abba, Father.**
> **16 The Spirit itself** [or Himself] **beareth witness with our spirit, that we are the children of God.**

If you are not born again, accept Christ as your Savior today!

Receiving the New Birth

The New Birth results in a *new creation* from above—the direct operation of the Word of God and the Spirit of God upon your life—changing your spirit completely when you truly repent and turn to God.

> **2 CORINTHIANS 5:17**
> **17 Therefore if any man be in Christ, he is a new creature: old things are passed away; behold, all things are become new.**

This *new creation* is brought about by following these steps:

1. Recognize that you are a sinner—lost, without God, and without hope (Rom. 3:23).

2. Admit that Jesus Christ died on the Cross to save you from sin by His own precious blood.

3. Come to God, turning away from sin and confessing Jesus as your Lord—*and you shall be born again.* (The Holy Spirit will then make you a new creature—a new creation—cleansing you from all sin by the authority of the Word of God and by the blood of Christ which was shed to atone for your sin.)

4. Believe from your heart and confess with your mouth that God does forgive you of your sins and that you are born again.

Believe and Confess

The following are some scriptures which show you what you have in your new authority in Christ. Believe and confess these scriptures.

ROMANS 10:9–10
9 That if thou shalt confess with thy mouth the Lord Jesus, and shalt believe in thine heart that God hath raised him from the dead, thou shalt be saved.
10 For with the heart man believeth unto righteousness; and with the mouth confession is made unto salvation.

JOHN 1:12–13
12 But as many as received him, to them gave he power to become the sons of God, even to them that believe on his name:
13 Which were born, not of blood, nor of the will of the flesh, nor of the will of man, but of God.

JOHN 6:37
37 . . . and him that cometh to me I will in no wise cast out.

Oh, what a basis for faith! There is no such thing as a person's coming to Him and being cast out! Jesus said, ". . . *him that cometh to me I will in no wise cast out*"!

JOHN 3:14–21
14 And as Moses lifted up the serpent in the wilderness, even so must the Son of man be lifted up:
15 That whosoever believeth in him should not perish, but have eternal life.
16 For God so loved the world, that he gave his only begotten Son, that whosoever believeth in him should not perish, but have everlasting life.
17 For God sent not his Son into the world to condemn the world; but that the world through him might be saved.
18 He that believeth on him is not condemned: but he that believeth not is condemned already, because he hath not believed in the name of the only begotten Son of God.
19 And this is the condemnation, that light is come into the world, and men loved darkness rather than light, because their deeds were evil.

20 For every one that doeth evil hateth the light, neither cometh to the light, lest his deeds should be reproved.
21 But he that doeth truth cometh to the light, that his deeds may be made manifest, that they are wrought in God.

JOHN 3:36
36 He that believeth on the Son hath everlasting life: and he that believeth not the Son shall not see life; but the wrath of God abideth on him.

JOHN 5:24
24 Verily, verily, I say unto you, He that heareth my word, and believeth on him that sent me, hath everlasting life, and shall not come into condemnation; but is passed from death unto life.

ACTS 3:19
19 Repent ye therefore, and be converted, that your sins may be blotted out, when the times of refreshing shall come from the presence of the Lord.

EPHESIANS 2:8-9
8 For by grace are ye saved through faith; and that not of yourselves: it is the gift of God:
9 Not of works, lest any man should boast.

You have the intelligence to see for yourself what the Bible says. Again, I warn, do not listen to the interpretations of men who will tear apart the simple Scriptures and leave you confused.

They do not care for your soul or they would not seek to rob you of your true Christian experiences.

If they had a love for you at all, they would at least permit you to believe the Bible just as it is. And they would encourage you to receive Bible experiences.

When they fight so hard to rob you of these benefits, you would be a fool not to "wake up" and see that they are agents of the devil in sending men to hell. It matters not that they are the most refined and wonderful religious men you have ever met—they are not ministers of God if they are robbing you of God's blessing.

The Bible says, *"And no marvel; for Satan himself is transformed into an angel of light. Therefore it is no great thing if his ministers also be transformed as the ministers of righteousness; whose end shall be according to their works"* (2 Cor. 11:14–15).

The Water of the New Birth

We read that Jesus said, *"Marvel not that I said unto thee, Ye must be born again"* (John 3:7). Just before He said that, He said, *". . . Verily, verily, I say unto thee, Except a man be born of water and of the Spirit, he cannot enter into the kingdom of God"* (John 3:5).

What is the *water* of the New Birth? What does it mean?

Does it refer to being baptized in water? Does that save you? No, that is not what Jesus is talking about.

The Word of God is the water referred to in John 3:5. Let's prove that by looking through a number of scriptures.

EPHESIANS 5:26
26 That he might sanctify and cleanse it with the washing of water by the word.

JOHN 6:63
63 It is the spirit that quickeneth; the flesh profiteth nothing: the words that I speak unto you, they are spirit, and they are life.

JOHN 15:3
3 Now ye are clean through the word which I have spoken unto you.

JOHN 17:17
17 Sanctify them through thy truth: thy word is truth.

1 PETER 1:23
23 Being born again, not of corruptible seed, but of incorruptible, by the word of God, which liveth and abideth for ever.

JAMES 1:18
18 Of his own will begat he us with the word of truth, that we should be a kind of firstfruits of his creatures.

One must believe what the Word of God says about man—that man is a sinner and that Christ died to save him from all sin. Then if man will confess his sins to God and turn from sin with a whole heart and believe the Gospel, he is conforming to the Word of God.

The Holy Spirit will then transform his life by the power of the Word of God and the blood of Christ. *That moment*, he is born again!

This new creation—the newly born child of God— is then to believe the Word of God and walk accordingly. He must begin to read the Bible and pray to God. He needs to walk and live in the Spirit and be conformed to the Word of God as he receives light.

Being born again—becoming the child of God—is of foremost importance. It is the key that unlocks all the promises of God to you. For when you become a child of God, then God's promises become yours.

New Creation Facts

Believers, Christians, the following are some Bible facts about the *new creation* that you are in Christ.

You Are a Child of God!

No truth in all the Bible is as far reaching as the blessed fact that when we are born again into the family of God—*God the Father is our Father.* He cares for us! He is interested in us, each of us individually, not just as a group or as a Body or a Church. He is interested in each of His children and loves each one of us with the same love.

Much is heard about the "fatherhood of God and the brotherhood of man," but Jesus said to some very religious people, *"Ye are of your father the devil . . ."* (John 8:44). God is the Creator of all mankind, but a man must be born again to become His child. He is God to the world, but Father only to the new creation man.

God is your very own Father. You are His very own child. And if He is your Father, you can be assured He will take a father's place and perform a father's part. You can be certain that your Father loves you and will take care of you. (*See* John 14:23; 16:23, 27; Matt. 6:8–9, 26, 30–34; 7:11.)

Get acquainted with your Father through the Word. When you were saved, you were born into His family as a spiritual baby. Babies in the natural must eat natural food to develop and grow. The Bible instructs the children of God: *"As newborn babes, desire the sincere milk of the word, that ye may grow thereby . . ."* (1 Peter 2:2). It is in the Word where we find out about our Father—about His love, His nature, how He cares for us, and how He loves us. He is everything the Word says He is. He will do everything the Word says He will do.

In Christ, you are a new creature—a new creation—a new species!

I'm glad I am a new creature. I was only fifteen, but I remember when it happened. Something took place inside of me. It seemed as if a two-ton load rolled off my chest. Not only did something depart from me—but something came into me. I was not the same person. There was a change inside.

In the New Birth, our spirits are recreated. (Our bodies are not. It is our spirit where all things have become new. We still have the same bodies we always had.) There is a man who lives inside the body. Paul calls him the *inward man* or the *spirit man*. He calls the body the *outward man*.

2 CORINTHIANS 4:16
16 For which cause we faint not; but though our outward man perish, yet the inward man is renewed day by day.

Peter calls this inner man *the hidden man of the heart* (1 Peter 3:4). This man is hidden to the physical eye. No one can see the real you—the inward man. They may think they do, but they only see the house (the body) you live in. You are on the inside looking out! The same thing is true with the people you know: You've never really seen the real man on the inside. You don't know what he looks like. You have only seen the house he lives in. When a man's house or body is decayed, the real man still lives. The real man never dies.

It is this inward man who becomes a new man in Christ, a new creation. It is the inward man who is born into the family of God, who becomes God's own child and who is in perfect union with the Master.

You Are One With the Master!

The believer and Jesus are one. Jesus said, *"I am the vine, ye are the branches . . ."* (John 15:5). When you look at a tree, you don't think of the branches as one part, and the rest of the tree as another part. You see it as one—as a union.

1 CORINTHIANS 6:17
17 But he that is joined unto the Lord is one spirit.

We are one with Christ. Our spirits are one with Him. Jesus is the Head; we are the Body.

All Things Are Possible to You!

No one argues with the scripture which says, *". . . with God all things are possible"* (Matt 19:26). Yet the same New Testament also says, *". . . all things are possible to him that believeth"* (Mark 9:23).

Are these scriptures equally true? Could one be a statement of fact and the other a misconception or falsehood? No! Both statements are *fact*.

All things are possible to him that believeth! It helps me as I drive down the road to say that. It helps me when I face a seemingly impossible situation to say aloud, "All things are possible to him that believeth. And I believe!"

The Greater One Is in You!

1 JOHN 4:4
4 Ye are of God, little children, and have overcome them: because greater is he that is in you, than he that is in the world.

Ye Are of God!

"Ye are of God" is another way of saying you are born of God. It says the same thing Second Corinthians 5:17 says—that if any man be in Christ, he is a new creation. John tells us in First John 4:4 that we are born of God—that we have been born again, that our spirits have been recreated, that we are *of God.*

Sadly, many Christians don't know they are born of God and that they have received eternal life (the life and nature of God). They think eternal life is something they are *going* to have one day when they get to Heaven. Many think they have simply received forgiveness of sins.

If we have been taught that our sins are just forgiven and that we will remain justified only if we walk carefully before God, and if we have never been taught that the nature and substance of God is within our spirits, then sin and Satan will continue to reign over us.

But when we know that the man on the inside, the real man, has been born again and is a new self in Christ Jesus, then we will rule and reign over Satan!

"Ye are of God, little children, and have overcome them: because greater is he that is in you, than he that is in the world" (1 John 4:4).

He that is in the world is the god of this world— Satan (2 Cor. 4:4). But, thank God, greater is He who is in us than the god of this world! Greater is He who is in us than Satan. He who is in us is greater than demons. He is greater than evil spirits. He is greater than sickness. He is greater than disease. He is the Greater One! And He lives in me! He lives in you! He who is *in yo*u is greater than any force you may come against.

2 CORINTHIANS 6:16
16 And what agreement hath the temple of God with idols? for ye are the temple of the living God; as God

hath said, I will dwell in them, and walk in them; and I will be their God, and they shall be my people.

How many Christians are conscious of the fact that God is dwelling in them? It sounds far-fetched, but what does this scripture mean if it does not mean what it says?

It is time for the Church to become "God-inside" minded! Too long it has been weakness-minded, sickness-minded, inferiority complex-minded, and trouble- and poverty-minded. That's all we've talked and thought about until a serious condition of doubt, unbelief, and spiritual failure has been created in the Church. This psychology of unbelief has robbed us of vibrant Christian faith and living, and of the abundant life Jesus intended that we should have.

JOHN 10:10
10 . . . I am come that they might have life, and that they might have it more abundantly.

When we know that the Life-Giver indwells us—that the Author of all life everywhere has condescended in the Person of His Son, through the power of the Holy Spirit, to come down and live within us—then our very beings shall radiate *life*!

"Greater is He that is in you than he that is in the world." Grasp that. You are of God. You are born

from above. The same mighty Spirit who raised Christ from the dead dwells in you (Rom. 8:11). It's no wonder the Bible says, ". . . *all things are possible to him that believeth*" (Mark 9:23). It is because the God with whom all things are possible lives within us through the New Birth!

— Chapter 2 —

Learning to Forget

Not as though I had already attained, either were already perfect: but I follow after, if that I may apprehend that for which also I am apprehended of Christ Jesus.

Brethren, I count not myself to have apprehended: but this one thing I do, forgetting those things which are behind, and reaching forth unto those things which are before,

I press toward the mark for the prize of the high calling of God in Christ Jesus.

—Philippians 3:12–14

There are two things I want you to notice about this passage that Paul wrote to the Church at Philippi: 1) "forgetting those things which are behind" and 2) "reaching forth unto those things which are before."

Forget the Past

Before you can go on with God, you must forget about the past. In this chapter, I will show you how

Paul, once known as Saul of Tarsus, had to forget about his past as a persecutor of Christians in order to minister effectively.

Let's notice something Paul said about himself in writing to Timothy:

1 TIMOTHY 1:11-16
11 According to the glorious gospel of the blessed God, which was committed to my trust.
12 And I thank Christ Jesus our Lord, who hath enabled me, for that he counted me faithful, putting me into the ministry;
13 Who was before a blasphemer, and a persecutor, and injurious: but I obtained mercy, because I did it ignorantly in unbelief.
14 And the grace of our Lord was exceeding abundant with faith and love which is in Christ Jesus.
15 This is a faithful saying, and worthy of all acceptation, that Christ Jesus came into the world to save sinners; of whom I am chief.
16 Howbeit for this cause I obtained mercy, that in me first Jesus Christ might shew forth all longsuffering, for a pattern to them which should hereafter believe on him to life everlasting.

The Word of God tells us that Saul was present at the stoning of Stephen.

ACTS 7:58
58 And cast him [Stephen] out of the city, and stoned him: and the witnesses laid down their clothes at a young man's feet, whose name was Saul.

And Saul consented to Stephen's death:

ACTS 8:1
1 And Saul was consenting unto his death. . . .

Turning further in the Acts of the Apostles, you can read an account that Luke, inspired by the Holy Spirit, wrote about Paul:

ACTS 9:1–2
1 And Saul, yet breathing out threatenings and slaughter against the disciples of the Lord, went unto the high priest,
2 And desired of him letters to Damascus to the synagogues, that if he found any of this way, whether they were men or women, he might bring them bound unto Jerusalem.

But, thank God, God's great mercy reached Paul! That's one thing he was talking about when he said, *". . . forgetting those things which are behind. . . . I press toward the mark . . ."* (Phil. 3:13–14). It would have been a terrible thing for Paul to continually remember the havoc he had wrought in the Church by consenting to the death of Stephen and persecuting believers.

Dear friend, if we are to be successful in our Christian life and ministry, there is one thing we must do—and it's a lesson Paul learned: *We must learn to forget.* If we don't learn this lesson, we'll be handicapped the rest of our life in living for God.

Remember this: The Lord Himself said in Isaiah— and it's repeated in the New Testament—*"I, even I, am he that blotteth out thy transgressions . . . and will not remember thy sins* [iniquities]" (Isa. 43:25). If *He* doesn't remember them, why should *you?*

Notice what God said in the next verse: *"Put me in remembrance . . ."* (v. 26). In other words, God is telling us to *remind* Him of what He said!

Why? You need to remind Him and yourself, because when you enter into the Presence of God to pray, the devil will bring all kinds of accusations against you. Invariably, he will bring your past before you as a photograph.

But that's all it is—just a picture! It doesn't exist anymore!

God said, "I've blotted it out." If He blotted it out, it doesn't exist.

Let's look again at verse 25: *"I, even I, am he that blotteth out thy transgressions for mine own sake, and will not remember thy sins."*

God didn't say He wouldn't remember your sins or iniquities for *your* sake (although you do receive the benefit of it); He said it was for *His* sake that He would not remember your sins. Why? So He can bless you. So He can help you. So He can demonstrate His great mercy and love on your behalf!

Looking further at Isaiah 43:26, we realize that this is an invitation from God to come before Him and state your case. It's talking about prayer: *"Put me in remembrance: let us PLEAD together: declare thou, that thou mayest be justified."*

Marginal notes in some Bibles say, "Set forth your case." And you can do that only when you learn to forget.

Coming over to the New Testament, we see a similar verse in Hebrews 8:12: *"For I will be merciful to their unrighteousness, and their sins and their iniquities will I remember no more."*

You can see that Paul had to forget his past in order to walk on with God and to stand in the full potential of the office and ministry God had called him to.

Learning to Forgive

Closely associated with learning to forget is *learning to forgive*. This forgiveness is twofold: Not only must you learn to forgive *others*; you also must learn to forgive *yourself.*

Notice what Jesus said about forgiveness in Matthew's Gospel.

MATTHEW 18:21
21 Then came Peter to him [Jesus], and said, Lord, how oft shall my brother sin against me, and I forgive him? till seven times?

Peter seemed to want to answer his own question. It was a good question, wasn't it? Is it pertinent today, or did it just apply to people living back then? This is what Jesus said:

MATTHEW 18:22
22 Jesus saith unto him, I say not unto thee, Until seven times: but, Until seventy times seven [that's 490 times!].

Now turn to Luke chapter 17. I want you to notice what Jesus says about the same question in verse 4.

LUKE 17:4
4 And if he trespass against thee seven times in a day, and seven times in a day turn again to thee, saying, I repent; thou shalt forgive him.

If you'll compare the two portions of Scripture, you'll see that "until seventy times seven" in Matthew and "seven times" in Luke applied to one *day*, not a lifetime!

Faith to Forgive

You see, we *hear* a lot preached about forgiveness, and we *talk* a lot about forgiveness. But somehow, we don't *practice* it the way the Bible said to. When you begin to study the subject in detail, it almost shocks you. Let's take a closer look at Luke 17.

LUKE 17:3–5
3 Take heed to yourselves: If thy brother trespass against thee, rebuke him; and if he repent, forgive him.
4 And if he trespass against thee seven times in a day, and seven times in a day turn again to thee, saying, I repent; thou shalt forgive him.
5 And the apostles said unto the Lord, Increase our faith.

This is still part of the faith message. It takes faith to forgive! In fact, your faith won't work unless you do forgive.

Remember in Mark 11:24, Jesus said, *". . . What things soever ye desire, when ye pray, believe that ye receive them, and ye shall have them."* Then with the same breath, in the same setting, He immediately began talking about forgiveness in connection with prayer: *"And when ye stand praying, forgive, if ye have ought against any: that your Father also which is in heaven may forgive you your trespasses"* (v. 25). He's talking about *prayer* in verse 24 and *forgiveness* in verse 25.

Now let's return to Matthew chapter 18, where we saw Peter asking, *". . . Lord, how oft shall my brother sin against me, and I forgive him? till seven times?"* (v. 21). Jesus answered him, *". . . I say not unto thee,*

Until seven times: but, Until seventy times seven"
(v. 22). Then Jesus went on to give a parable that
illustrates what He's talking about.

MATTHEW 18:23–32
23 Therefore is the kingdom of heaven likened
unto a certain king, which would take account of
his servants.
24 And when he had begun to reckon, one was
brought unto him, which owed him ten thousand
talents [or probably well over $10,000,000 in our money
today].
25 But forasmuch as he had not to pay, his lord com-
manded him to be sold, and his wife, and children,
and all that he had, and payment to be made.
26 The servant therefore fell down, and worshipped
him, saying, Lord, have patience with me, and I will
pay thee all.
27 Then the lord of that servant was moved with
compassion, and loosed him, and forgave him
the debt.
28 But the same servant went out, and found one
of his fellowservants, which owed him an hundred
pence: and he laid hands on him, and took him by
the throat, saying, Pay me that thou owest.
29 And his fellowservant fell down at his feet, and
besought him, saying, Have patience with me, and I
will pay thee all.
30 And he would not: but went and cast him into
prison, till he should pay the debt.
31 So when his fellowservants saw what was done,
they were very sorry, and came and told unto their
lord all that was done.
32 Then his lord, after that he had called him, said
unto him, O thou wicked servant. . . .

Why did the king call the servant *wicked*? Because he wasn't willing to forgive. There's no use in discussing what's more or less wicked. If it's wicked, we don't want to have anything to do with it!

Let's continue reading.

MATTHEW 18:32–35
32 . . . I forgave thee all that debt, because thou desiredst me:
33 Shouldest not thou also have had compassion on thy fellowservant, even as I had pity on thee?
34 And his lord was wroth, and delivered him to the tormentors, till he should pay all that was due unto him.
35 So likewise shall my heavenly Father do also unto you, if ye from your hearts forgive not every one his brother their trespasses.

That's plain enough, isn't it?

Whether you realize it or not, to forgive and to forget go hand in hand.

These are the things that hinder us from receiving from God, from growing spiritually, and from being who and what God wants us to be.

In June 1939, Oretha and I were moving our meager belongings into the little three-room parsonage of a church I'd just been called to pastor when one of the church members stopped by. She talked a little about the weather and different things, but, finally, she blurted what she had really come for. She said, "Now,

Brother Hagin, I know you're going to hear about it, and I wanted to tell you first so you could get it *first hand.*" (Usually, you'd better watch people like that!)

She said, "I wanted to tell you how old Sister So-and-so treated me." And she went on to tell me all about it.

Finally, I interrupted and asked, "When did this happen?" (I thought that during the ten days between the time the former pastor left and the time I arrived, they had gotten into a fuss, and their love had waxed cold for one another.)

She answered, "Let's see—*one, two, three, four, five, six, seven, eight* . . ." I thought she was going to say, "Eight days ago." Instead, she said, "This Thursday, I believe it will be eight years ago that it happened."

I guess my mouth fell open and my eyes got big. I was so surprised.

The woman said, "Oh, now, don't you misunderstand. I've forgiven her, all right, but you know, I never will forget how that old devil treated me!"

Without thinking, I pointed my finger right in her face and said, "Sister, you're a liar. If you had forgiven her, you'd have forgotten it. Now the devil might bring you a picture of it, but if you've *forgotten* it, you wouldn't be here talking about it."

Several months later, another member of the church came to the parsonage for a visit. After talking about other things, she finally said, "Brother Hagin, I've got a question for you."

"Well, fine," I said, "I'll answer it if I can."

She asked why members of her husband's family never failed to be healed, while members of her family, who seemingly were more spiritual, never had received healing in almost a quarter of a century.

I answered her, "Without knowing your husband's family, I would say, based on knowing the Bible, that they must have these characteristics: They are quick to *repent*; quick to *forgive*; and quick to *believe*."

When I said that to her, her mouth fell open and she batted her eyes like a frog in a west Texas hailstorm!

She said, "Why, that's exactly right! You've hit the nail right on the head!"

"No," I replied, "I didn't hit the nail on the head; God did. I got that from the Bible."

She said, "I believe my husband's family are the quickest people to repent, forgive, and believe that I've ever seen. In fact, some of them would stay out of church a long time, but when they did come to the altar, they'd repent the fastest, believe the quickest, and get blessed the most of anybody I've ever seen."

(Friends, there's something about believing God, like Smith Wigglesworth said, that will cause God to pass over a million people to get to you.)

Then the woman started telling me about her family. She said, "I believe we're the slowest people you've ever seen when it comes to forgiving. We will forgive eventually, but the only reason we do is because we know we *have* to, not because we *want* to. And I believe we're the slowest people you've ever seen when it comes to believing."

So we can see the importance of forgiving others in order to receive the blessings of God. But there's more to it than just forgiving others.

Forgive *Yourself*

Another thing that hinders people is that they're often unwilling to forgive themselves. And that's just as wrong as it is not to forgive others.

Years ago, I was holding a meeting in Fort Worth, and a woman asked me to pray for her. At first, she was reluctant to tell me her problem.

I told her, "How am I going to have faith for something if I don't know what I'm having faith for? I can't. Or how am I going to agree on something when I don't even know what I'm agreeing on?"

"You won't laugh at me, will you?"

"No," I said. "I might laugh *with* you, but I won't laugh *at* you."

"Well," she said, "my husband is unsaved. We were married a number of years before I came to this church and got born again and filled with the Holy Spirit.

"Before I got saved, I was always hot-tempered— just real fiery. I'd just 'go off,' you know. But for this entire eight years, I've been able to hold that in.

"A while back, my husband came in one Saturday night and acted like he was drunk. He never has drunk much in all the years we've been married. He's not a Christian, but he's a fine gentleman. I love him, and he loves me. He's just not saved yet.

"But some way or other, I got mad—my temper got away from me—and I started hitting him, and he started hollering, 'I'm not drunk; I'm not drunk! I'm just putting on! I only had two drinks! I just thought it would be fun to come in and *pretend* I was drunk.'"

She said, "That made me even madder, and I mean, I let him have it with 'both barrels.' Then I went to my room and slammed the door.

"After I cooled off, I felt so embarrassed, because I had said a lot of things I shouldn't have. I got down on my knees and prayed nearly all night long, 'Dear God, forgive me. Oh, my God, forgive me!'

"Then the next morning at the breakfast table, I said to my husband, 'Honey, I want you to forgive me. I've prayed nearly all night long, and I know God said in His Word that He'd forgive me. But I want you to forgive me too.'"

She continued, "My husband said, 'Well, if anybody ought to ask anybody to forgive, *I* ought to ask *you*. I started the whole thing; I'm the culprit.'

"'Yes,' I said, 'but I'm a Christian and you're not. I just blew my stack and said a lot of things I shouldn't have—in fact, I don't even know everything I said and did.'

"'No,' he said, 'I'm entirely to blame. You forgive me.' Finally, Brother Hagin, we agreed to forgive *one another*."

"Well," I said, "you haven't turned in any prayer request yet. What is it you want us to pray about?"

She replied, "I wanted you to pray that God will give me some kind of *feeling* so I'll know He's forgiven me."

I started laughing. I couldn't keep from it!

"Sister," I said, "do you know what you've just told me? You've just told me that you've got more faith and confidence in your unsaved husband than you do in God. You asked your husband to forgive you, and he did. You both agreed you'd forgive one another. And that settled it, didn't it?"

"Yes," she said. "It did."

"But you won't take God at His Word. He said if we'll confess our sins, He's faithful and just to forgive us of our sins and to cleanse us from all unrighteousness [1 John 1:9]. Why don't you take Him at His Word?

"When your husband said, 'Forgive me—I'm to blame,' did you get off the chair, get on your knees, and say, 'Now, Lord, give me some kind of feeling so I'll know my husband has really forgiven me'? No, you just forgave your husband, and he forgave you. Do you have more confidence and more faith in your unsaved husband and *his* word than you do in *God's* Word?"

Then I said, "Do you know what your problem is?"

She said, "Do *you*?"

I said, "I sure do."

She said, "Tell me, then."

I said, "You're unwilling to forgive *yourself* over the fact that you lost your temper. God's forgiven you. You've forgiven your husband. Your husband has forgiven you. But you haven't forgiven *yourself*—you keep holding that against yourself. Forgive yourself, and you'll feel all right. You won't have to pray that God will give you any kind of a feeling."

Several days later, she returned, and I didn't have to ask her anything. Her face looked like a neon sign turned on in the dark! She was all smiles because she had forgiven herself!

You've got to take that first step.

You can't press toward the mark for the prize of the high calling of God in Christ Jesus without forgetting the things that are behind. And to forget them means to *forgive*—not only others but yourself.

You see, we're to forgive like God does. Remember Ephesians 4:32? It says, *". . . be ye kind one to another, tenderhearted, forgiving one another, even as God for Christ's sake hath forgiven you."*

How does God forgive? He forgets. Forgiving and forgetting go hand in hand.

Some people haven't done that yet. If you need to forgive others, do it. But also forgive yourself of past mistakes, failures, and faults.

I remember there was a certain businessman in a meeting I was holding, and I laid hands on him three times for healing, but he didn't get healed. All the leading healing evangelists of that day had laid hands on him; he'd been in all their meetings.

He told me he'd had a heart attack and that he had a severe kidney condition. His doctors had told him to sell his business. They said if he stayed on medication and rested, he might live another two years. He was only fifty-four years old. I agreed to meet him in the pastor's study.

On the way to our meeting, it was as if someone were sitting in the back seat of my car. I realized it was the Lord talking to me.

He said, "Do you think I'd require you to do something I wouldn't be willing to do?"

I said, "Why, no, Lord. You wouldn't do that. If You required me to do something and You weren't willing to do it, that would be unjust. And You're not unjust."

Again, that Voice said, "Do you think I would require you to do something I wouldn't be willing to do?"

"No, Lord," I said, "You wouldn't do that. If You required me to do something and You were not willing to do the same thing, that would be unjust. And You're not unjust; You're just and righteous."

A little while later, He asked me the third time: "Do you think I would require you to do something I wouldn't be willing to do?"

"No," I answered. "You wouldn't do that—that would be unjust!"

Then He said, "Do you think I'd require you to forgive your brother if he turned, repented, and said,

"'Forgive me'" 490 times in one day—if *I* wasn't willing to do it?"

I said, "Certainly, You'd be willing to do it." (That's what got me to thinking and studying along this line. I had to look it up, and when I put the scripture references together, I could see He was talking about forgiving 490 times in one day.)

When I got to church, I found out why the Lord had told me this. In our counseling session, the businessman said, "Brother Hagin, I've been saved and baptized with the Holy Spirit for thirty-five years. I've been prayed for by every outstanding healing evangelist in America. I've missed it in so many ways. I've failed so often in this thirty-five-year period."

I was ready for him. God had gotten me ready for him.

I asked him, "Do you think God would require you to do something He wouldn't be willing to do?"

"No, of course not," he replied.

I brought to his attention the fact that he hadn't forgiven himself for the mistakes he'd made over the past thirty-five years. When he forgave himself, I laid hands on him to pray for his healing. He realized that God would freely forgive him when he repented and asked Him to (he wasn't sure before). Then he was healed.

Years later, I was preaching in that area, and some of this man's relatives told me he had retired from business the previous year. They said, "He was seventy-five years old and got tired of running his business. He just decided he'd get out of it and go fishing for a while."

Hindrances like unforgiveness stand in the way of healing for many people, even though they search, seek, and ask others to pray for them. Until they correct their thinking, healing won't work for them.

But if believers will purpose to forget those things in the past, to forgive others, and to forgive themselves as God has forgiven them, they will be in a position to receive the blessings of God in their lives.

— Chapter 3 —

The Bible Experience of Receiving the Holy Spirit

The infilling of New Testament believers with the Holy Ghost should be our pattern today. I propose that we look at the Acts of the Apostles, see how they did it, and follow their example in getting people filled with the Holy Ghost.

In the first chapter of Acts, just before Jesus ascended on high, Jesus gave certain instructions concerning this infilling of the Holy Ghost.

> **ACTS 1:4–5**
> **4 And, being assembled together with them, [Jesus] commanded them that they should not depart from Jerusalem, but wait for the promise of the Father, which, saith he, ye have heard of me.**
> **5 For John truly baptized with water; but ye shall be baptized with the Holy Ghost not many days hence.**

And then on the Day of Pentecost, we see this great scene:

> **ACTS 2:1–4**
> **1 And when the day of Pentecost was fully come, they were all with one accord in one place.**
> **2 And suddenly there came a sound from heaven as of a rushing mighty wind, and it filled all the house where they were sitting.**

3 And there appeared unto them cloven tongues like
as of fire, and it sat upon each of them.
4 And they were all filled with the Holy Ghost, and
began to speak with other tongues, as the Spirit gave
them utterance.

Many years ago as a young denominational pastor
reading the New Testament, I was enlightened concerning this Pentecostal experience. The Holy Spirit
enlightened and convinced me that if I received the
same Holy Ghost they received, I would have the same
initial sign they had—Bible evidence—and that is
speaking with tongues. I wasn't satisfied with anything
else. Speaking with tongues is not the Holy Ghost. And
the Holy Ghost is not the speaking with tongues. But
they go hand in hand.

Believers Filled in Samaria

The events in the Book of Acts cover a number of
years. Eight years after the Day of Pentecost, we see
Philip carrying the Gospel to the people of Samaria.

ACTS 8:5–8, 12
5 Then Philip went down to the city of Samaria, and
preached Christ unto them.
6 And the people with one accord gave heed unto
those things which Philip spake, hearing and seeing
the miracles which he did.
7 For unclean spirits, crying with loud voice, came
out of many that were possessed with them: and

many taken with palsies, and that were lame, were healed.
8 And there was great joy in that city. . . .
12 But when they believed Philip preaching the things concerning the kingdom of God, and the name of Jesus Christ, they were baptized, both men and women.

These scriptures helped me to see that there is an experience subsequent to salvation called receiving the Holy Ghost. I had been taught that when you are saved, you have the Holy Ghost, which is true in a sense. But my denomination taught that you had all the Holy Ghost there was when you were born again.

Jesus said, ". . . *Go ye into all the world, and preach the gospel to every creature. He that believeth and is baptized shall be saved; but he that believeth not shall be damned*" (Mark 16:15–16). These Samaritans believed and were baptized (Acts 8:12). Were they saved? According to Jesus they were.

There is a work of the Holy Spirit in the New Birth, but that is not called receiving the Holy Ghost—that is called being born again, receiving eternal life. There is an experience following salvation called receiving or *being filled with* the Holy Ghost.

When the apostles at Jerusalem heard of the wonderful things God had done through Philip's ministry in Samaria, they sent Peter and John to lay hands on the new converts that they might receive the Holy Ghost.

> ACTS 8:14–17
> 14 Now when the apostles which were at Jerusalem heard that Samaria had received the word of God, they sent unto them Peter and John:
> 15 Who, when they were come down, prayed for them, that they might receive the Holy Ghost:
> 16 (For as yet he was fallen upon none of them: only they were baptized in the name of the Lord Jesus.)
> 17 Then laid they their hands on them, and they received the Holy Ghost.

Now some who object to speaking with tongues argue that the Bible doesn't mention that the Samaritans spoke with tongues when they received the Holy Ghost. But it doesn't say they *didn't!* Students of Church history know that the Early Church fathers agree that they did speak with tongues in Samaria. And it also seems apparent from this passage that they did speak with tongues.

> ACTS 8:18–19
> 18 And when Simon [the sorcerer] SAW that through laying on of the apostles' hands the Holy Ghost was given, he offered them money,
> 19 Saying, Give me also this power, that on whomsoever I lay hands, he may receive the Holy Ghost.

The Word says, ". . . *when Simon SAW.* . . ." Well, you can't see the Holy Ghost. He is a Spirit and cannot be seen with the physical eye. Then what did Simon see? There had to be some physical sign whereby Simon would know they had received the Holy Ghost—something which would register on Simon's senses. All evidence indicates the sign manifested was speaking in tongues.

Believers Filled in
Cornelius' Household

About ten years after the Day of Pentecost the Word tells us that Peter went to Cornelius' house to carry the Gospel.

> ACTS 10:44–46
> 44 While Peter yet spake these words, the Holy Ghost fell on all them which heard the word.
> 45 And they of the circumcision which believed were astonished, as many as came with Peter, because that on the Gentiles also was poured out the gift of the Holy Ghost.
> 46 For they heard them speak with tongues, and magnify God. . . .

Reading the entire account of this, we see that an angel appeared to Cornelius and told him to "send to Joppa" and to inquire for Peter in the house of a certain individual *"Who shall tell thee words, whereby thou and all thy house shall be saved"* (Acts 11:14). Neither Cornelius nor his household was saved. They were Jewish proselytes. A person can't be saved without hearing the Gospel.

The members of Cornelius' household didn't know about Jesus, so Peter preached to them. As Peter preached, they believed while they were standing there and were born again. Then they received the Holy Ghost and spoke in tongues before Peter finished his message!

Notice that it was the speaking with tongues that convinced Peter's company that these Gentiles had received the Holy Spirit. The Jewish believers were astonished that the Holy Spirit was poured out on the Gentiles!

Believers Filled in Ephesus

Then twenty years after the Day of Pentecost, Paul journeyed to Ephesus. There he met some believers and introduced to them the Person of the Holy Ghost.

ACTS 19:1–3, 6
1 And it came to pass, that, while Apollos was at Corinth, Paul having passed through the upper coasts came to Ephesus: and finding certain disciples,
2 He said unto them, Have ye received the Holy Ghost since ye believed? And they said unto him, We have not so much as heard whether there be any Holy Ghost.

> 3 And he said unto them, Unto what then were ye baptized? And they said, Unto John's baptism. . . .
> 6 And when Paul had laid his hands upon them, the Holy Ghost came on them; and they spake with tongues, and prophesied.

As we see from the preceding verses, these believers at Ephesus had never heard about the Holy Ghost. But when Paul laid his hands on them, the Holy Ghost came upon them, and they spoke with tongues. Every one of them—without waiting, praising, or tarrying—was filled with the Holy Ghost and spoke with other tongues as the Spirit of God gave them utterance.

Paul's Infilling of the Spirit

Paul, who laid hands on these folks, was previously known as Saul of Tarsus. The account of his experience of receiving the Holy Ghost is found in the ninth chapter of Acts.

> ACTS 9:10–12, 17
> 10 And there was a certain disciple at Damascus, named Ananias; and to him said the Lord in a vision, Ananias. And he said, Behold, I am here, Lord.
> 11 And the Lord said unto him, Arise, and go into the street which is called Straight, and inquire in the house of Judas for one called Saul, of Tarsus: for, behold, he prayeth,
> 12 And hath seen in a vision a man named Ananias coming in, and putting his hand on him, that he might receive his sight. . . .

17 And Ananias went his way, and entered into the house; and putting his hands on him said, Brother Saul, the Lord, even Jesus, that appeared unto thee in the way as thou camest, hath sent me, that thou mightest receive thy sight, and be filled with the Holy Ghost.

Saul, later to be known as Paul, received the Holy Ghost immediately. He didn't have to tarry or wait. He received instantly.

"But it doesn't say that he spoke with tongues," someone might object. That is true; it doesn't say it specifically right here. But Paul himself said that he spoke with tongues. He said, *"I thank my God, I speak with tongues more than ye all"* (1 Cor. 14:18). We know Paul didn't start talking with tongues before he received the Holy Ghost. It shouldn't be too difficult to figure out when he started! He started when he received the Holy Ghost, just as the rest of us did, for the tongues go along with the experience.

Speaking with tongues is an initial supernatural sign or evidence of the Holy Spirit's indwelling. It is the beginning of it all. I have found in my own life that the more I pray and worship God in tongues, the more manifestation of other gifts of the Spirit I have. The less I talk in tongues, the less manifestations I have. Speaking with tongues is the door into the rest of the spiritual gifts (1 Cor. 12:1–11).

— Chapter 4 —

Why Tongues?

Ten Reasons Why Every Believer Should Speak in Tongues

And these signs shall follow them that believe; In my name shall they cast out devils; they shall speak with new tongues.

—Mark 16:17

The Apostle Paul wrote much about the subject of speaking in other tongues. He apparently practiced what he preached, for he said, *"I thank my God, I speak with tongues more than ye all"* (1 Cor. 14:18). I, too, thank God that I speak in tongues with regularity, and would wish for every believer this same blessing and source of power in his everyday life. The purpose of this chapter is to set forth major reasons why every Christian should speak in tongues and to help believers see the blessings that can be theirs through appropriating the power of the Holy Spirit daily.

Reason 1: Tongues—The Initial Sign

ACTS 2:4
4 And they were all filled with the Holy Ghost, and began to speak with other tongues, as the Spirit gave them utterance.

The Word of God teaches that when we are filled with the Holy Ghost, we speak with other tongues as the Spirit of God gives utterance. It is the initial evidence or sign of the baptism of the Holy Spirit. Therefore, the first reason people should speak with other tongues is, *it is a supernatural evidence of the Spirit's indwelling.*

In the tenth chapter of Acts, we read where the Jewish brethren who came with Peter to Cornelius' house were astonished when they saw that the gift of the Holy Ghost was poured out on the Gentiles. They thought it was just for the Jews. How did these Jews know that Cornelius' household had received the gift of the Holy Ghost? *"For they heard them speak with tongues, and magnify God . . ."* (Acts 10:46). Speaking in tongues was the supernatural sign which convinced them that the Gentiles had the same gift they had.

Reason 2: Tongues Are for Spiritual Edification

1 CORINTHIANS 14:4
4 He that speaketh in an unknown tongue edifieth himself. . . .

In writing to the Church at Corinth, Paul encouraged them to continue the practice of speaking with other tongues in their worship of God and in their prayer lives as a means of spiritual edification. (Notice it is not for mental nor physical edification.) Greek language scholars tell us that we have a word in our modern vernacular which is closer to the original meaning than the word "edified." That word is "charge," as used in connection with charging a battery. Therefore, we could paraphrase this verse, "He that speaketh in an unknown tongue edifies, charges, builds himself up like a battery." And this wonderful, supernatural means of spiritual edification is for every one of God's children.

> 1 CORINTHIANS 14:2
> 2 For he that speaketh in an unknown tongue speaketh not unto men, but unto God: for no man understandeth him; howbeit in the spirit he speaketh mysteries.

Moffatt's translation of this verse says, "He speaks divine secrets." God has given to the Church a divine, supernatural means of communication with Himself!

> 1 CORINTHIANS 14:14
> 14 For if I pray in an unknown tongue, my spirit prayeth, but my understanding is unfruitful.

Notice that this says, "my spirit prayeth." The *Amplified* translation reads, "my spirit [by the Holy Spirit within me] prays."

God is a Spirit. When we pray in tongues, our spirit is in direct contact with God, who is a Spirit. We are talking to Him by a divine, supernatural means.

It is amazing how people can ask in the light of these scriptures, "What is the value of speaking in tongues?" If God's Word says speaking in tongues is of value—then it is of value! If God says that it edifies—then it edifies! If God says it is a supernatural means of communication with Himself— then it is! If God says every believer should speak in tongues—*then every believer should speak in tongues!* Jesus said, *"And these signs shall follow them that believe . . ."* (Mark 16:17). "Them" is plural—it means *all.* And one of the signs was, *". . . they shall speak with new tongues"* (v. 17).

Reason 3: Tongues Remind Us of the Spirit's Indwelling Presence

JOHN 14:16–17
16 And I will pray the Father, and he shall give you another Comforter, that he may abide with you for ever;
17 Even the Spirit of truth; whom the world cannot receive, because it seeth him not, neither knoweth

him: but ye know him; for he dwelleth with you, and shall be in you.

Howard Carter, who was general supervisor of the Assemblies of God in Great Britain for many years and founder of the oldest Pentecostal Bible school in the world, pointed out that we must not forget that speaking with other tongues is not only the *initial* evidence of the Holy Spirit's infilling, but is a *continual* experience for the rest of one's life. For what purpose? To assist us in the worship of God. Speaking in tongues is a flowing stream which should never dry up, and will enrich the life spiritually.

Continuing to pray and worship God in tongues helps us to be ever-conscious of His indwelling Presence. If I can be conscious of the indwelling Presence of the Holy Ghost every day, it is bound to affect the way I live.

A minister's twelve-year-old daughter once lost her temper and was talking rudely and hatefully to her mother. A visiting evangelist overheard the scene. When the girl looked up and saw him, knowing he had witnessed her tantrum, she was embarrassed and broke into tears.

"I'm so sorry you saw me act this way and heard what I said," she cried.

"Honey," he said, "there is One greater than I who saw you and heard you. You are a Christian, aren't you?"

"Yes."

"And filled with the Spirit?" he asked.

"Yes."

"Well then, the Holy Ghost is in you. He knows what you said and how you acted. But if you will repent, the Lord will forgive you."

They prayed together. She repented, and in a little while began to worship God in tongues.

Then he said to her, "Here is a secret that will help you curb your temper. If you will pray and worship God every day in tongues, it will help you to be conscious of the indwelling Presence of the Holy Ghost. If you will remember that He is in you, you won't act that way."

Some years later, the evangelist returned to preach at that church, and the pastor's daughter told him, "I have never forgotten what you said. Every day for the past few years, I have prayed and worshipped God in tongues—and I have never lost my temper again."

Unfortunately, we all know people who have been filled with the Holy Ghost, yet still lose their temper and say and do things they shouldn't. This is only because they haven't been walking in the Spirit as they should. It is so easy, when we are not conscious of His Presence, to become irritated and frustrated. But if we will take time to fellowship with Him, we can be ever-conscious of His indwelling Presence.

Reason 4: Praying in Tongues Is Praying in Line With God's Perfect Will

ROMANS 8:26–27
26 Likewise the Spirit also helpeth our infirmities: for we know not what we should pray for as we ought: but the Spirit itself [or Himself] **maketh intercession for us with groanings which cannot be uttered.**
27 And he that searcheth the hearts knoweth what is the mind of the Spirit, because he maketh intercession for the saints according to the will of God.

Speaking in tongues keeps selfishness out of our prayers. A prayer out of one's own mind and thinking has the possibility of being unscriptural. It may be selfish. Too often our prayers are like the old farmer's, who prayed, "God bless me, my wife, my son John, his wife—us four and no more."

In the scriptures quoted above, Paul didn't say we didn't know *how* to pray, for we do: We pray to the Father in the Name of the Lord Jesus Christ, which is the correct way to pray (John 14:13–14; 15:16; 16:23–24, 26). But just because I know how to pray doesn't mean I know for what to pray as I ought. Paul said, *". . . we know not what we should pray for as we ought: but the Spirit itself* [Himself] *maketh intercession for us with groanings which cannot be uttered"* (Rom. 8:26).

P.C. Nelson, a scholar of the Greek language, said that the Greek literally reads here, "The Holy Ghost maketh intercession for us in groanings that cannot be uttered in articulate speech." Articulate speech means our *regular kind of speech.* He went on to point out how the Greek stressed that this not only includes groanings escaping our lips in prayer, but also praying in other tongues. This agrees with what Paul said in First Corinthians 14:14, *"For if I pray in an unknown tongue, my spirit prayeth. . . ."* Or, as the *Amplified* translates, "My spirit [by the Holy Spirit within me] prays."

When you pray in tongues, it is your spirit praying, by the Holy Spirit within you. The Holy Spirit within you gives the utterance, and you speak it out of your spirit. You do the talking; He gives the utterance. By this method, the Holy Spirit helps you pray according to the will of God—as things should be prayed for.

This isn't something the Holy Ghost does apart from us. Those groanings come from inside us and escape our lips. The Holy Ghost isn't going to do our praying *for* us. He is sent to dwell in us as a Helper and an Intercessor. He isn't responsible for our prayer lives—He is sent to *help* us pray.

Praying with other tongues is praying as the Spirit gives utterance. It is Spirit-directed praying. It eliminates the possibility of selfishness in our prayers.

Many times when people have prayed out of their own minds, they have received things that were actually not the will of God and were not best. If God's people insist on having things a certain way, even if it isn't best for them, or it is not God's perfect will, He will often permit it. God did not want Israel to have a king, but they kept insisting that they wanted one. So He permitted them to have one (*see* First Samuel 8:5–22; 10:19). But it was not His perfect will.

Reason 5: Praying in Tongues Stimulates Faith

JUDE 20
20 But ye, beloved, building up yourselves on your most holy faith, praying in the Holy Ghost.

Praying in tongues stimulates faith and helps us learn to trust God more fully. If the Holy Spirit supernaturally directs the words I speak, faith must be exercised to speak with tongues. For I don't know what the next word will be; I am trusting God for it. And trusting God along one line will help me to trust Him in another.

As a young Baptist minister, I pastored a community church and stayed in the home of a Methodist couple. The wife was a fine, dear woman who loved the Lord. But she had an ulcerated stomach, which doctors feared would lead to cancer. Her husband made good money, but he had spent everything he had on medical bills. I knew God could and would heal her, but, somehow, I was never able to lift her faith up to that point. She ate only soft foods and milk and had difficulty keeping that on her stomach. But one day a wonderful thing happened! She received the infilling of the Holy Spirit. When I came in, she was eating foods she'd never been able to eat.

"I received not only the baptism of the Holy Ghost and spoke with other tongues," she told me, "but I received my healing too. I'm perfectly well." And she was.

I've seen this happen many times. What is the connection? We know that receiving the baptism of the Holy Ghost does not heal us. However, speaking with tongues helps us to learn how to trust God more fully. Speaking in tongues helps us believe God for other things in that it stimulates or charges our faith.

Reason 6: Speaking in Tongues Is a Means of Keeping Free From Worldly Contamination

1 CORINTHIANS 14:28
28 But if there be no interpreter, let him keep silence in the church; and let him speak to himself, and to God.

The sixth reason every Christian should speak in tongues is that this is a means of keeping free from the contamination of the ungodly and the profane, and all the vulgar talk around us on the job or out in public.

Notice from the scripture above that we can speak with tongues to ourselves. Paul said that in the church service, *"If any man speak in an unknown tongue, let it be by two, or at the most by three, and that by course; and let one interpret. But if there be no interpreter, let him keep silence in the church; and let him speak to himself, and to God"* (1 Cor. 14:27–28).

If we can speak to ourselves and to God in a church service, we can also do it on the job. It won't disturb anyone. In the barber shop, for instance, when men tell risque jokes, I just sit there and speak to myself and to God in tongues. Riding the train, bus, or airplane—we can speak to ourselves and to God. Talking in tongues to ourself and to God will be a means of keeping free from contamination.

Reason 7: Praying in Tongues Enables Us to Pray for the Unknown

Praying in tongues provides a way to pray for things for which no one thinks to pray or is even aware of. The Holy Spirit helps us pray, for "we know not how to pray as we ought" (Rom. 8:26). But in addition, the Holy Spirit, who knows everything, can pray through us for things about which our natural minds know nothing.

An English missionary to Africa was home on furlough speaking at a missionary conference when a woman asked him if he kept a diary. He replied that he did. She began to relate to him, "About two years ago, I was awakened in the night with a burden to pray. I got out of bed and was talking in tongues before I got down on my knees. Then for an hour, I prayed in tongues, and it seemed as if I were wrestling. When I finished praying I had a vision. I saw you in a little grass hut, surrounded by natives. You were sick. Then you died. I saw the natives pull the sheet over your head and walk sadly outside the hut. Suddenly, you came out of the hut and stood in their midst, and all the natives rejoiced."

This woman also kept a diary. The missionary requested she bring it that afternoon. Comparing diaries, and making allowances for time differences in England and Africa, they discovered the time of the woman's prayer burden exactly coincided with the time when the missionary was sick with a deadly fever. His partner was away, and he was alone with the natives. Things happened just as she saw them. The missionary died, the natives saw him die and pulled a sheet over his head. Then he rose up suddenly well! Why did this happen? Because of the Spirit of God!

In 1956 when my wife and I were in California, I was awakened suddenly in the night. It was as if someone laid his hand on me. I sat bolt upright in bed, my heart beating rapidly.

"Lord," I cried, "what is the matter? I know something is wrong somewhere. Holy Spirit within me, You know everything. You are everywhere as well as within me. Whatever this is, You give me utterance."

I prayed in tongues for an hour and then began to laugh and sing in tongues. (When praying this way, always continue praying until you have a note of praise. Then you will know that whatever it is you are praying about, is settled.) I knew what I had been praying for had come to pass. I had the answer, so I went back to sleep.

I dreamed that I saw my youngest brother become extremely ill in Louisiana. I saw an ambulance with flashing lights take him to the hospital. In the dream, I stood in the corridor outside his hospital room door. The door was shut. Then the doctor came out that door, pulled it shut behind him, shook my hand and said, "He is dead."

"No, doctor, he is not dead," I replied.

"What do you mean, 'He is not dead'?"

"The Lord told me he would live and not die."

At that, the doctor became angry and said, "Come with me, and I will show you that he is dead. I have pronounced too many people dead not to know when someone is dead." He took me by the arm and led me into my brother's room. He walked over to the bed and jerked the sheet back. When he did, my brother's eyes opened. The doctor saw that he was breathing. He began to stutter, "You knew something I didn't know. He is alive, isn't he?"

In that dream I saw my brother rise up from the bed, well. That was what I had been praying about.

Three months later, we came home to Texas. My youngest brother came by to see me and said, "I nearly died while you were gone." I told him that I knew he'd had an attack during the night while staying in a motel in Louisiana and that he had been rushed to the hospital. He thought someone had told me about it, but they had not. I told him about my burden of prayer, followed by the dream.

"That's exactly how it happened! They told me that for about forty minutes at the hospital, the doctor thought I was gone."

Praying in the Spirit provides a way for things to be prayed for that we wouldn't know anything about in the natural. The Holy Ghost, however, knows everything.

Reason 8: Praying in Tongues Gives Spiritual Refreshing

ISAIAH 28:11–12
11 For with stammering lips and another tongue will he speak to this people.
12 To whom he said, This is the rest wherewith ye may cause the weary to rest; and this is the refreshing: yet they would not hear.

What is the rest, the refreshing, the above scripture refers to? Speaking in other tongues!

Sometimes the doctor recommends a rest cure, but I know the best one in the world. Often when you take a vacation, you have to come home and rest before going back to work! But isn't it wonderful that we can take this "rest cure" every day? "*. . . This is the rest . . . this is the refreshing . . .*" (Isa. 28:12). We need this spiritual refreshing in these days of turmoil, perplexity, and anxiety.

Reason 9: Tongues Are
for Giving Thanks

1 CORINTHIANS 14:15-17
**15 What is it then? I will pray with the spirit, and
I will pray with the understanding also: I will sing
with the spirit, and I will sing with the understanding also.**
**16 Else when thou shalt bless with the spirit, how
shall he that occupieth the room of the unlearned
say Amen at thy giving of thanks, seeing he under-
standeth not what thou sayest?**
**17 For thou verily givest thanks well, but the other is
not edified.**

When Paul said in verse 16, "... *he that occupieth
the room of the unlearned ...,*" he was referring to
those who are unlearned in spiritual things.

If you invited me to dinner and said, "Please give
thanks"; and if I prayed in tongues, you wouldn't
know what I said. You wouldn't be edified. Therefore, Paul said it would be better to pray with
your understanding in such cases. If I did pray in
tongues, I should interpret it so everyone would
know what was said.

But notice that Paul says praying in tongues
provides the most perfect way to pray and to give
thanks, for he said, "Thou givest thanks well" (v. 17).

In the presence of people who are unlearned,
however, Paul said to pray with your understanding

so that they can be edified and understand what you say.

Reason 10: Speaking in Tongues Brings the Tongue Under Subjection

JAMES 3:8
8 But the tongue can no man tame; it is an unruly evil, full of deadly poison.

Yielding the tongue to the Holy Spirit to speak with other tongues is a giant step toward fully yielding all of our members to God. For if we can yield this most unruly member, we can yield any member.

The Public Side of Tongues

In conclusion, I want to point out that, while we have dealt primarily with tongues in the individual believer's private life, it is also true there is a public side to tongues.

First, when people receive the Holy Ghost publicly, they speak with other tongues as the Spirit gives utterance.

Secondly, the church is edified by speaking with other tongues in the public assembly with interpretation. Paul plainly stated that to prophesy is to speak unto men ". . . *to edification, and exhortation, and comfort*" (1 Cor. 14:3). But he said, ". . . *greater is he that prophesieth than he that speaketh with tongues, except he interpret . . ."* (1 Cor. 14:5).

Paul was saying that tongues with interpretation is equivalent to prophecy. For example, if the utterance in tongues is interpreted so that the church can understand what is said, then the one prophesying is not greater.

To illustrate this point, two nickels equal one dime. However, the two nickels are not a ten-cent piece. Prophecy is the dime, the ten-cent piece. Naturally, it would be better to have the dime (prophecy) than to have the nickel (an utterance in tongues). But if interpretation (another nickel) went along with it, then the two would be equivalent to the dime.

Let me say here that prophesying is not preaching. If prophesying were preaching, then you wouldn't have to make any preparation to preach. But you have to study and prepare to preach. Paul said, *"Study to shew thyself approved unto God . . ."* (2 Tim. 2:15). You don't have to study to speak with tongues or to interpret. You don't have to study to prophesy. These come by inspiration of the Spirit. Of course, when one is preaching under the inspiration of the Spirit, and suddenly he says things he never thought of, that is inspiration, and there is an element of prophecy to that.

Tongues with interpretation edifies the church. When used in line with the Word of God, speaking with tongues with interpretation convinces the unbeliever of the reality of the Presence of God, and often causes him to turn to God and be saved.

Jesus said, *"And these signs shall follow them that believe; In my name shall they cast out devils; they shall speak with new tongues"* (Mark 16:17). This, too, can be both private and public.

Of course, we don't want prolonged praying in tongues in the service, because unless there is an interpretation, folks don't know what is said and are not edified. It is all right to pray in the altar service as long as you want, for you go there to be edified. If people in the service are lifting their hands and praying, it is all right to pray in tongues. I stand on the platform and pray that way every night. But when the congregation ceases praying, I cease praying. The congregation wouldn't be edified if I went on and on.

We do need to know how to use what we have to the greatest advantage.

— Chapter 5 —

The Importance of Words

Talked to 'Death' or 'Life'?

Jesus Himself said, *"For by thy WORDS thou shalt be justified, and by thy words thou shalt be condemned"* (Matt. 12:37).

When I was meditating on this subject, one word from this text kept going over and over in my spirit, and that was the word "words." Something on the inside of me seemed to impress me to teach on *words*. Words are more important than a lot of people realize.

Words make us or break us. *Words* heal us or make us sick.

According to the Bible, words destroy us or make us full of life, happiness, and health.

Our words—the words we spoke yesterday—made life what it is today.

That agrees with what Jesus said in Mark 11:23: *"For verily I say unto you, That whosoever shall SAY unto this mountain, Be thou removed, and be thou cast into the sea; and shall not doubt in his heart, but shall believe that those things which he SAITH shall come to pass; he shall have whatsoever he SAITH.*"

You could read that verse like this: "He shall have whatsoever—the *words*—he speaks."

In June 1943, I was starting a meeting for a certain pastor in the east Texas oil fields. He'd had a serious heart attack. One of the neighboring pastors told me, "Brother Hagin, for two or three days, the doctor tried to get us to quit praying for Pastor _____. He was between life and death, and the doctor said, 'You're holding him here by your prayers and faith. If he does revive, which I doubt he will, his mind will never be right, because blood didn't get to his brain for more than ten minutes.'

"But we just couldn't stop praying for him," this other pastor said. "We kept praying. The third day, Pastor _____ revived, and his mind was all right. The doctors were shocked."

Pastor _____ had not resumed preaching yet. His wife, who was also a minister, was filling the pulpit. My wife and I and our children stayed in the parsonage with them, and we all went to church in one car.

One night, Pastor _____ started to make an announcement in the service, and he said it backwards. The minute he got into the car after the service, his wife said, "Well, you made a mess of that.

It's just like the doctor said; I guess you will have to quit preaching."

My wife spoke up and said, "There is nothing wrong with Kenneth's mind, yet he did worse than your husband did. Kenneth got his tongue tangled up three times tonight while ministering."

But the pastor's wife continued to say to her husband, "You'll have to quit preaching." She was constantly telling him what he couldn't do.

One day after we ate our main meal, my wife went to the beauty shop and Pastor _____ went to visit someone who was sick, so I helped the pastor's wife with the dishes. As we were standing there washing and drying the dishes, the Lord inspired me to say, "Sister, I don't know how you're going to take this, but if you don't quit talking like you do to your husband, he'll be dead in two years. You're going to talk him to death!"

She flared up at me, and I said, "Now, wait just a minute, Sister. Wait just a minute! You know that wasn't Kenneth Hagin who said that. The Spirit of God inspired me to tell you that. I would stake my life on it."

So she simmered down and said, "Brother Hagin, we've known you for a number of years, and we know how God uses you, so I'll accept that as being from the Lord."

While we were there, she did better. A year later, we were visiting them again, and she was right back to her old ways, talking "death" to her husband, saying, "You're going to die; you'll never make it!"

I tried to get her to stop, but she just shook her head "no" and wouldn't listen to me.

Then, a few months later, I was holding a revival for a friend who was currently pastoring Pastor _____'s church. While I was in that revival, the other ministers came and preached his funeral. I compared notes, and it was almost exactly two years from the day I'd had that word for his wife. She talked her husband to death!

After this pastor's death, Mrs. _____ became angry at God because her husband died. She never preached another sermon. She backslid, and as far as I know, their children never lived for the Lord. Thank God, the husband went to Heaven.

All of that happened because of *words*.

As a sixteen-year-old Baptist boy lying on a bed of sickness, I received the revelation of God's Word. I began by acting on Mark 11:23 and 24, saying, "I believe."

Words were spoken.

I said, "I believe I receive healing for my deformed heart.

"I believe I receive healing for the incurable blood disease.

"I believe I receive healing for the paralysis.

"I believe I receive healing from the top of my head to the soles of my feet!"

And within the hour, I was standing on my feet!

I had learned the secret of *words*—*faith* words.

More than sixty years have come and gone, and I haven't had a headache —not one. The last headache I can actually remember having was in August 1933.

I haven't had a headache, and I'm not expecting to have one. But if I had a headache, I wouldn't tell anyone. And if someone asked me how I was feeling, I would say, "I'm fine, thank you."

I would speak the right *words*, because Jesus said in Mark 11:23, "*. . . he shall have whatsoever he saith.*" I believe what the Word of God says in Isaiah 53:5: "*. . . with his stripes we are healed.*"

I believe that. I believe that I am healed.

How Your Words Can Affect
Your Children

When Ken Jr. was just two and a half hours old, I held that little fellow up in my hands and said, "Lord, thank You for this boy. I realize that You've given to my wife and me this new life that I hold in my hands. I realize that he's my responsibility, because I know the Bible. It says to train up this child in the way he should go, and when he is old, he will not depart from it [Prov. 22:6].

"I realize that Your Word says to bring children up in the nurture and admonition of the Lord [Eph. 6:4], and I'm going to do it. I'm going to do it, because children are trained not only by precept, but also by example. I'm going to live right in front of him. I'm going to do what's right. And I'll be honest with You and him if I miss it."

When our little girl, Pat, was born, I took her into my hands immediately, and said the same thing over her that I'd said over Ken: "I'll do right; I'll raise her right. I'll train her. I'll set the right example in front of her and teach her precepts from the Word of God. I will also teach her by example.

"I know you can have what you say, so I say that this child, like Ken, will grow up strong physically, without sickness or disease. She will be alert mentally and stalwart spiritually."

Years afterward, even our kinfolk, who felt we had ruined everything by going off with that "tongue-talking bunch," said to us, "There is something to that; there *has* to be. Your children are never sick."

I never prayed in my life that either of my children would be saved—not one single prayer. I never prayed a prayer that either one of them would be filled with the Spirit. They're adults now with families of their own, and I don't believe I prayed more than half a dozen times for both of them in all these years.

Why? Because you can have what you say—and I had already said it! If I were to pray about it now, it would mean that I didn't mean what I said back then. But I did mean it, because I know I can have what I say. And both Ken and Pat got saved and filled with the Spirit at an early age.

In raising our children, sometimes if I lost my temper, I had to go to them and say, "Forgive me; Daddy acted ugly." I had to say, "I've set the wrong example. I've asked the Lord to forgive me, and He's forgiven me. Will you forgive me?"

And those little children would say, "All right."

I never told my children not to do something "just because I told you not to." I sat down and read the Bible to them, proving to them that I had their interests at heart.

If I had to reprimand them or even spank them, I said, "It says right here in Ephesians 6, *'Children, obey your parents in the Lord: for this is right. Honour thy father and mother; (which is the first*

commandment with promise;) That it may be WELL
with thee, and thou mayest live long on the earth'"
(vv. 1–3).

I explained to them that days that a person is sick
or in the hospital are not well days. I said, "You see,
I want it to be well with you. I want you to enjoy long
years on the earth."

Children are a product of words!

As I said, words heal us or make us sick.

Words bless us or curse us.

The words that I hear in the morning will linger
with me all through the day.

Some wives little realize that a biting, stinging
word in the morning will rob a husband of efficiency
the whole day long. But a loving, tender, beautiful
word will fill him with music and lead him into
victory.

Learn to make words work for you. Learn to fill
words with power that cannot be resisted. The way
you fill words with power that cannot be resisted is
to fill words with love and faith.

Parents need to realize that the home atmosphere
is a product of *words!*

In 1958, as my wife and I were driving near Los
Angeles, she suggested, "Why don't we stop and see
Brother and Sister So-and-so?" We had held a revival

for them several months before, and their house was only about three blocks off the freeway.

"All right," I said, "we'll drive by."

We pulled up in the driveway, but we didn't see any activity. I rang the doorbell and heard someone coming. The pastor opened the door, shook hands with me, and I motioned for my wife to come inside.

The pastor said, "Brother Hagin, we were resting. My wife will have to dress. Just sit here in the living room." He had his robe on, so he went off to dress too. My wife came inside. She didn't see or speak to him.

The moment we sat on that couch, we turned to one another and said at the same time, "Sharp words were spoken in this home!"

The atmosphere was bad. We both sensed it immediately. Spiritual things are created by words. Even natural, physical things are created by words. For example, if you went into a room where someone had just been frying fish, you could smell the fish. The odor would still be in the atmosphere.

Well, the air was "heavy" in that room where my wife and I sat. The words were still in the air. (There are words in the air around you right now. If you don't believe it, turn on a transistor radio whereby words can be transmitted via airwaves.) As we talked to this pastor and his wife, we learned that they had indeed had a disagreement.

The lives and personalities of children brought up in that kind of an atmosphere will be warped. Mothers and fathers: Your home atmosphere is the product of words! Children fail because wrong words were spoken; the *right* words were *not* spoken in that home.

Why is it that some families grow up strong and win life's fight? It is because the right kind of words were spoken in the home.

My wife and I were visiting in New Mexico once on our day off. We drove more than one hundred miles to see friends who had just built a beautiful new church.

As they were showing us the new building, the pastor's wife was chatting with my wife, and she said, "You know, we can't do a thing in the world with our oldest boy. He's almost seventeen. He won't come to church. He wants to join the Navy, and when he turns seventeen, we're going to sign for him and let him go just to get rid of him. I guess you know what I'm talking about, though. You've got a teenage boy."

My wife replied, "No, I don't know what you're talking about. You'd have to knock our boy in the head to keep him out of church, even when he probably should stay home to study."

Why? Because he had been trained that way. The right kind of words were spoken in the home. Words make a child love an education. Words bring a child to church or keep him away. We are a product of *words*.

You can go to church on Sunday and sit there looking pious if you want to. You can pray and sing in the choir, and even teach Sunday school. But if you fly off the handle at home and cuss, fuss, and "raise the devil," as we'd say in Texas, you're going to lose your children! Why? Because children are not brought up in a church atmosphere; they're brought up in a *home* atmosphere. And that church atmosphere on Sunday is going to affect them very little if the atmosphere at home is not right.

One Sunday morning during the summer of 1943, I was preaching at a church in north central Texas. My text was Colossians 2:9 and 10, where it says "ye are complete in him," and my title was "What Is Spirituality?" I have never been brave enough to use that text again.

I asked the question: "Where would you go to look for a spiritual person?"

Some thought of people in our church who were quick to jump, dance, and shout, and they said, "Those people are spiritual."

I told the congregation, "That's not spirituality. You can't judge spirituality by that."

Someone else said, "So-and-so is always talking in tongues and giving messages in tongues, so he's *really* spiritual."

I said, "No, no. You can't judge spirituality by that, because God will use any kind of vessel He can. I read where He talked through a donkey one time [Num. 22:23–30]! That doesn't mean that donkey was spiritual.

"No," I said. "I know that spiritual people do go to church, but I wouldn't even go to church if I were looking for a spiritual person. You know the first place I'd go?"

They all said, "No."

I said, "I'd go to a person's home."

You see, when it comes to religious things, people can be two-faced. They've got one face they wear on Sunday, and another face they wear another day. As a pastor, I've seen people like this. I've knocked on their doors and have heard them whisper, "Put that up! It's Brother Hagin!" There was something they didn't want me to see. You never heard such scurrying around! In one case, I remember I thought they were never going to open the door!

"No," I told that congregation, "I'd just like to become the invisible man, walk through the door of a person's home, and look and listen. People who are spiritual—people who have really got something—

live right when they're at home, not just when they're in church."

If you don't live right at home, you haven't got anything!

A lady in the second pew said, "Oh, my God, that leaves me out!" (She later said she thought she had only *thought* about saying that; she didn't realize she actually said it out loud!)

It ruined my sermon. Everyone burst out laughing. I fell over the pulpit, laughing. I stopped right there, and I've never tried preaching that sermon again.

'The Tongue of the Wise Is Health'

Have you ever visited the sick? Have you ever listened to them talk? If you have, many times you can find out why they are sick.

Proverbs 12:18 is a wonderful revelation, a marvelous truth: *"There is that speaketh like the piercings of a sword: but the tongue of the wise is health."* You are not going to *have* health unless you *talk* health.

Did you ever notice that we are programmed wrong? (I'm talking from the natural standpoint.) We are programmed negatively.

The Bible says, *"Blessed is the man that walketh not in the counsel of the ungodly . . ."* (Ps. 1:1). You do not want to think like the world thinks.

Romans 12:1 says, *"I beseech you therefore, brethren, by the mercies of God, that ye present your bodies a living sacrifice, holy, acceptable unto God, which is your reasonable service."*

Now notice verse 2: *"And be not conformed to this world: but be ye transformed by the renewing of your mind . . . ."* God does not want you to be conformed to this world, but to be transformed. How? By the renewing of your mind. Do not think like the world thinks. They think negatively.

We have read Romans 12:2, however, and thought it was saying, "Don't do things that people in the world do." Well, there are a lot of things you do that they do. You eat like they eat, usually, and you sleep like they sleep. This verse is primarily talking about renewing your mind and thinking like God thinks according to the Word, not like the world thinks.

Several years ago, I was holding a meeting in a certain church in Oklahoma. This particular group thought women were going to hell unless they wore long sleeves, long dresses, and long hair. They always talked about "worldliness."

"We're not to be conformed to the world," they said. "The Bible said, 'Be not conformed.' We're not going to be worldly around here."

The pastor of this church had asked me to preach on Sunday morning. I woke up several times throughout Saturday night, and each time I did, I was praying about the message. "God, I don't preach this way, ordinarily," I said, as I saw what the sermon was to be. But God really dealt with me.

That morning I jumped off the platform, ran up and down the aisles, and said, "I'll tell you, this is the most *worldly* church I've ever preached in!"

It was as if I had slapped them in the face with a wet dish rag! Here I was saying that this was the most worldly church I'd ever been in—and they were bragging about how *holy* they were!

They were like the Pharisees. They prayed, "Lord, we're better than anyone else in town. We're just the greatest and the best. We're the most wonderful people. Of course, we know that You know that. We don't do this; we don't do that; we don't do something else." But they were the most negative bunch I had ever seen.

I said, "You still think just like the world. You think sickness. You think fear. You think doubt. You think defeat. You think failure—just like the world thinks! Get your mind renewed with the Word of

God! *Think* in line with God's Word! *Talk* in line with God's Word! *Believe* in line with God's Word!"

Many people who think they are so separated from the world are sometimes the most worldly people of all. As I said, the whole world is programmed negatively, and if you are not careful, you will make the same mistake the world does. You see, the world without God is in spiritual death. They are programmed to death instead of life.

If a person is frightened, he will say, "That just scares me *to death*. I'm scared to death."

Never say that. I never say that I am scared, because I am not.

If I am tempted to be fearful, I speak to it. I say, "Fear, I resist you in Jesus' Name!" I refuse to fear. And if doubt comes, I speak to it. I say, "Doubt, I resist you in Jesus' Name!" I refuse to doubt.

I wouldn't tell anyone if I had a "fear" thought, or a "doubt" thought. I wouldn't accept it. I wouldn't tell someone if the thought came to me to fear or doubt— and you know the devil can put all kinds of thoughts in your mind.

We are a product of words. Did you ever stop to think that the Bible teaches that there is health and healing in your tongue? Did you notice that He said, "The tongue of the wise is health" (Prov. 12:18)?

I never talk sickness; I don't believe in sickness. I talk health. *The tongue of the wise is health.* The Bible does not say, "The tongue of the wise is *sickness.*" It says, *". . . the tongue of the wise is HEALTH"* (Prov. 12:18).

I talk health. I believe in healing; I believe in health. I never talk sickness; I never talk disease. I talk health and healing.

I never talk failure; I don't believe in failure. I believe in success. I never talk defeat; I don't believe in defeat. I believe in winning! Hallelujah to Jesus!

I never talk about what the devil has done. I'm not interested in his works. I talk about the works of God and what He is doing, praise the Lord! I don't talk about the devil's power, because he is not as powerful as God.

One night, a preacher on TV spent his whole sermon talking about what the devil's doing. I thought to myself, *Dear Lord, I'm going to turn that off!* And I turned it off right in the middle of his exposé of ignorance! The longer he talked, the worse I felt. He never told anyone anything they didn't already know. And besides that, he was bragging on the devil.

By the way that TV preacher talked, you'd have thought poor old God had gone out of business—that He'd lost all of His power. You'd have thought that all Christians were going to have to go through life with their noses to the grindstone, sick and afflicted and living on Barely-Get-Along Street way down at the end of the block, right next to Grumble Alley, singing, "If I can just make it in." There was no message of victory or success in this man's sermon.

Jesus said, "I will be with you always" (Matt. 28:20). I believe that if He is with me—*that's* success!

The Bible says in Romans 8:31, ". . . *If God be for us, who can be against us?*" Oh, glory to God, if He is for us, what difference does it make who's against us? What difference does it make what the devil's doing out in the world? God is *for* us! He is on our side!

In First John 4:4 it says, ". . . *greater is he that is in you, than he that is in the world.*" What do you care what you face if the Greater One is in you?

I've been tempted to worry, just like everyone else, but I don't worry. I never talk discouragement. I never talk worry. I never talk defeat.

Some people get delivered from smoking cigarettes, and some people get delivered from drinking whiskey or alcohol, but I wish Christian people would get delivered from the biggest sin—a sin greater than smoking cigarettes or drinking whiskey—and that is the sin of worry.

A lot of people are so proud. They say, "I don't smoke; God delivered me from that." Well, I wish they would get delivered from that other sin they have in their life. The sin of worry is worse than smoking a cigarette.

Smoking and drinking are wrong. I am not in favor of either of them, and I don't have either of those bad habits. But worry is worse than either one of them.

Worry will kill you. More than one doctor has said to me (and I've read it in periodicals), "There are more people in mental institutions and in the grave because of worry than any other thing."

What do people worry about? Circumstances. They worry about tomorrow. They worry about the things they face.

I've been tempted to worry about tomorrow and about things I've faced. But then I remembered who the Bible said is inside of me. I didn't even have to pray about it. I just looked trouble and seeming impossibilities in the face, and I couldn't keep from laughing, praise God!

I said, "If I don't make it over you, I'll make it around you. If I don't make it around you, I'll make it under you. If I don't make it under you, I'll make it through you—because the Greater One is in me!"

And, you know, while I was laughing, that circumstance went off and hid!

The Greater One is in me! Greater is He who is in you than he that is in the world (1 John 4:4). Well, who is in the world? The devil is the god of this world (2 Cor. 4:4). What else is in the world? Sin is in the world. But the Greater One is in me. He's greater than sin. He conquered sin; He put away sin (Heb. 9:26).

What else is in the world? Sickness is in the world. It's not of God. It doesn't come from Heaven. There's no sickness up there; it's of this world. There won't be any sickness in Heaven. The Greater One is in me. He's greater than sickness, because He's the Healer.

What else is in the world? Trouble is in the world. People are always talking about the trouble that's in this old world. But He who is in me is greater than the trouble that's in the world!

What else is in the world? Adverse circumstances are in the world. Seeming impossibilities are in the world. But I'm not of the world. I may be in the world, but I'm not of the world (John 17:11–18). My citizenship is in Heaven, glory to God! And while I'm down here in the world, I have the Greater One living in me. He is greater than he that is in the world. He will put me over. He will make me a success. Hallelujah, I cannot be defeated!

That's my confession. Words. Those are the kinds of words that I have been speaking for more than sixty years. Words, words, words!

What Is Your Confession?

PROVERBS 18:21
21 Death and life are in the power of the tongue: and they that love it shall eat the fruit thereof.

PROVERBS 21:23
23 Whoso keepeth his mouth and his tongue keepeth his soul from troubles.

MATTHEW 12:37
37 For by thy words thou shalt be justified, and by thy words thou shalt be condemned.

MARK 11:23
23 For verily I say unto you, That whosoever shall say unto this mountain, Be thou removed, and be thou cast into the sea; and shall not doubt in his heart, but shall believe that those things which he saith shall come to pass; he shall have whatsoever he saith.

For years, faith has been taught in the Church. People have been encouraged to believe. But we have not heard much teaching about *words* or *saying what you believe.*

The preceding scriptures illustrate the importance of words. Another such verse is Hebrews 4:14: *"Seeing then that we have a great high priest, that is passed into the heavens, Jesus the Son of God, let us hold fast our profession."*

The word translated "profession" in the *King James Version* is the same Greek word translated "confession" elsewhere.

In the margin of my Bible opposite this verse is the note "in the Greek, *confession.*" I looked up this word in the Greek concordance, read other translations, and found that the Greek text actually says, ". . . Let us hold fast *to saying the same thing.*"

Notice again that *words* are involved.

More than sixty years ago, as a Baptist boy on the bed of sickness, I began to understand Mark 11:23: ". . . *whosoever shall say . . . and shall not doubt in his heart, but shall believe that those things which he saith shall come to pass; he shall have whatsoever he saith.*" In other words, he will have the *words* he speaks!

Born and reared a Southern Baptist, I was taught to believe for salvation and to believe the Bible. When I saw these truths in Mark 11:23, I believed them. The thing that had kept me bedfast for sixteen months was not knowing how to turn my faith loose.

You won't get the blessings of God just because you have faith. You won't get healed or baptized in the Holy Spirit just because you have faith. You won't get answers to prayer just because you have faith. Most Christians think they will, but they are wrong. The Bible does not teach that.

The Bible teaches that you get saved because you believe *and say something*—not just because you believe.

> **ROMANS 10:9–10**
> 9 That if thou shalt confess with thy mouth the Lord Jesus, and shalt believe in thine heart that God hath raised him from the dead, thou shalt be saved.
> 10 For with the heart man believeth unto righteousness; and with the mouth confession is made unto salvation.

Not only does your heart have something to do with your salvation, your *mouth* has something to do with it too. *Words* have something to do with it.

The Bible does not say simply that if you believe in your heart that God raised Jesus from the dead, you will be saved. You will not be saved just because you believe it. Notice in verse 10, the phrase *". . . with the mouth. . . ." With the mouth* confession is made unto salvation.

> **MARK 11:23**
> 23 . . . whosoever . . . shall not doubt in his heart, but shall believe that those things which he saith shall come to pass; he shall have whatsoever he saith.

Jesus did not teach in Mark 11:23, "he shall have whatsoever he *believeth*." He taught, "he shall have whatsoever he *saith*." In other words, you will have what you speak. You will have your words.

Faith is always expressed in words. Faith must be released in words *through your mouth*. We can see that in all of these scriptures we read. When you *speak* something, that is putting *action* to it. It took me a long time to discover that—sixteen months of being bedfast—because no one had ever taught me that.

I'm not talking about the words you speak in church or the words you use when you pray. I'm talking about the words you use in your everyday life: the words you speak at home, with your friends, or at work. These everyday words do three things *to* you and *for* you:

1. The words you speak *identify* you.

2. The words you speak *set the boundaries of your life*.

3. The words you speak *affect your spirit* (your inward man).

If you want to locate yourself, just listen to the words you speak.

You'll never realize beyond your *words*. To put it another way, Jesus said in Mark 11:23, ". . . *he shall have whatsoever he SAITH*."

The thing that defeats a lot of people is their double confession. One time they will confess one thing, and the next time, they will confess something else.

If you talk to them, they will say, "Yes, the Lord is my Shepherd; I shall not want. Yes, I know that it says in Philippians 4:19, '. . . *my God shall supply all your need according to his riches in glory by Christ Jesus,*' and I'm believing God to supply my needs."

But then they will see someone else down the block, in the store, or at church. They will have their mind on their problem, and they will say, "Well, we're not doing too well. We're so far behind in our bills, we're about to lose our car and everything else."

What about that other confession? This second confession nullified the first.

Learn to hold fast to saying the same things. Remember, in the Greek, Hebrews 4:14 literally says, "Let us hold fast *to saying the same thing.*"

Never, never, never give up! No, it's not easy. If you're looking for something easy, you might as well give up and crawl in a hole and die.

The Bible said to *"fight"* (1 Tim. 6:12). I think that's as far as some people read. They started fighting. They thought that meant fighting other churches or fellow Christians. No, that's not what it meant. First Timothy 6:12 says we're to fight the good fight of *faith.*

In this fight, you've got to fight all of your physical senses—you've got to resist what they're telling you. Sometimes you've got to fight what all of your relatives say. Sometimes you've got to fight what the pastor says. Sometimes you've got to fight what all the church members say. Sometimes you've got to fight what a Sunday school teacher says. I know; I've been there.

There were times I made a confession and had to ignore what everyone else was saying. It was a fight to do it, because they were all telling me I was wrong and that it wouldn't work. It did work; it *does* work!

Too many people are looking for someone to do something for them. I can't fight your fight, and you can't fight my fight. You'll have to fight your *own* fight.

Your words are so important. You need to realize that. They set the boundaries of your life. *You will never realize anything beyond the words you speak. You will never have anything beyond your own words.*

— Chapter 6 —

In Him: Understanding
Who You Are in the Family

Faith Demands Expression
and Testimony

Testimony is part of the faith life, including your testimony of who you are *in Him*—in Christ. If you want to develop robust faith, then continually tell what the Lord is doing for you. The more you talk about it, the more real He becomes to you. The less you talk about it, the less real He will be to you.

Faith is like love; it is of the heart, the spirit. And like love, it lives and finds its joy in the continual confession of it. In the natural, the more a husband and wife confess their love for each other, the more their love grows.

If you'll notice carefully the life of Jesus, you'll find that from the beginning of His public ministry until He was led to the Cross, He was ever confessing *who* He was, *what* He was, and *His mission in life.*

For instance He said, *"I came forth from the Father, and am come into the world: again, I leave the world, and go to the Father"* (John 16:28). This was a fourfold confession. It covers His life from the Incarnation to the Ascension.

One of the boldest confessions Jesus made was, *". . . he that hath seen me hath seen the Father . . ."* (John 14:9). What a bold confession—"If you want to see the Father, look on Me"! In John 12 it is recorded that He said, *". . . he that seeth me seeth him that sent me. I am come a light into the world, that whosoever believeth on me should not abide in darkness"* (vv. 45–46).

Let me say it again. Jesus constantly confessed *who* He was, *what* He was, and *His mission in life.*

"Yes," someone might say, "but that was Jesus."

I know. And the Bible teaches that Jesus left us an example that we should follow in His steps. You should constantly be confessing who you are. Oh, no, not who you are physically—the son or daughter of John Doe who lives on Such-and-such Street—but who you are according to the Word of God. That's the confession we're to hold fast to (Heb. 4:14).

1 JOHN 3:1–2
1 Behold, what manner of love the Father hath bestowed upon us, that we should be called the sons of God . . .
2 Beloved, now are we the sons of God. . . .

ROMANS 8:14, 16–17
14 For as many as are led by the Spirit of God, they are the sons of God. . . .

16 The Spirit itself [or Himself] beareth witness with
our spirit, that we are the children of God:
17 And if children, then heirs; heirs of God, and joint-
heirs with Christ. . . .

We are children of God! Sons of God! We're heirs
of God—joint-heirs with Christ! We joyfully confess
our relationship with God. And in what way are we
related to Him? We're born of God. We're children
of God. He is our very own Father. We are His very
own children. We dare to take our place as sons and
daughters of God and confess that's who we are!

Find Out What God's Word Says
About You and Make That
Your Confession!

People often ask me about studying the Bible.
Although I have many suggestions, here is the one I
present above all others everywhere I go.

As a Christian, as a believer, read through the
New Testament—primarily the Epistles. (The Epistles are the letters written to you the believer. They
are written to the Church.) As you read, look for all
expressions such as, "in Christ," "in Him," "in whom,"
"through whom," etc. With a colored pencil, underline
these expressions. You will find approximately 140
such expressions, most of them in the Epistles. Some
of these, however, don't exactly tell you something you

have "in Christ." For instance, Paul's greeting in one Epistle is, "I greet you in the Name of the Lord Jesus Christ." That has the expression "in Christ" but it doesn't tell you anything that is yours because you are in Christ.

You will also find other scriptures which convey the same message, but do not use the specific phrases "in Him," etc. Yet they tell you *who you are* or *what you are* and *what you have* because you are in Christ.

Now, when you find these scriptures, write them down. Then meditate on them. Begin to confess them. Begin to say with your mouth, "This is who I am; this is what I am. And this is what I have—in Christ."

For, you see, faith's confessions create realities. As far as God is concerned, everything you have or are in Christ is so. He has done it. Everything the Bible says is ours, is ours legally. The Bible is a legal document, sealed by the blood of Jesus. However, it is your believing it and your confessing it which makes it a reality to *you*. God wants us to enjoy and know the reality of what He has provided for us—and His Word tells us how to do it!

As an example, we can see that God has provided the New Birth for us. And His Word tells us how that salvation can become real to us. Even though we sometimes talk like this, "God saved So-and-So last night," we know that from *God's* viewpoint, He didn't save that person just the previous night. He saved him back when Jesus was raised from the dead. The man just *accepted* his salvation "last night," and the redemption God had provided nearly two thousand years before became a reality to him.

> **HEBREWS 9:12**
> 12 Neither by the blood of goats and calves, but by his own blood he entered in once into the holy place, having obtained eternal redemption for us.

Jesus never has to do that again. He has already done it. The provision has been made. And Romans 10:10 tells us how we obtain the reality of salvation in our individual lives.

> **ROMANS 10:10**
> 10 For with the heart man believeth unto righteousness; and with the mouth confession is made unto salvation.

It is always with the heart that man believes— and with his mouth he makes his confession *unto* the reality of whatever it is he is believing. When you believe a thing in your heart and confess it with your mouth, then it becomes real to you. Faith's confessions create realities.

As you read some of the "in Christ," "in Him," and "in whom" scriptures, they won't seem real to you at first. It may not seem as though you really have what these scriptures say you have in Him. But if you will begin to confess with your mouth, because you do believe God's Word in your heart, "This is mine. This is who I am. This is what I have," then it will become reality to you. It is already real in the spirit realm. But we want it to become real in this physical realm where we live in the flesh. So remember as you find these scriptures to do the following:

1. Underline each scripture.

2. Write it down.

3. Meditate on it.

4. Make a confession of it.

5. Begin saying it "with your mouth" (not just thinking it in your heart).

'In Him' Realities
The Great Confession

Of course, the first confession we must make is the confession of Jesus as our Lord. Being born again, becoming a child of God, is the key which unlocks all of God's provisions and promises to us.

ROMANS 10:9–10
9 . . . if thou shalt confess with thy mouth the Lord Jesus, and shalt believe in thine heart that God hath raised him from the dead, thou shalt be saved.

10 For with the heart man believeth unto righteousness; and with the mouth confession is made unto salvation.

Confession: "I believe in my heart that Jesus Christ is the Son of God. I believe He was raised from the dead for my justification. I confess Him as my Lord and Savior. Jesus is my Lord. He is dominating my life. He is guiding me. He is leading me."

This confession changes our lordship. It defines our position. The confession of the Lordship of Jesus immediately puts us under the care and protection of the Lord Jesus Christ. He is our Shepherd. We have confessed Him as Lord, so we can go a step further and confess Him as Shepherd. The Twenty-Third Psalm now belongs to us. Jesus said, *"I am the good shepherd . . ."* (John 10:14).

I wake up in the mornings sometimes confessing, "The Lord is my Shepherd. I do not want. I do not want for ability. I do not want for strength. I do not want for money. I do not want for anything. The Lord is my Shepherd."

ACTS 17:28
28 For IN HIM we live, and move, and have our being. . . .

Confession: "In Him I live, and move, and have my being! What a vast storehouse of power! In Christ my Savior and Lord, I have Life! I have energy! I have strength for even the impossible tasks!"

JOHN 15:5, 7
5 I am the vine, ye are the branches. . . .
7 If ye abide **IN ME**, and my words abide in you, ye shall ask what ye will, and it shall be done unto you.

Confession: "I abide in Him. I live in Him. He is the Vine—I am the branch. The vine is in the branch—and the branch is in the vine. His life—the life of God—is in me. His nature—the love nature—is in me. Just as blood flows through my natural body, His life flows through my inner man. I will let that life and love dominate me."

When one is born again, he comes into Christ. That is the only way you can get "in Him." But then Jesus said, "If My words abide in you . . ." (John 15:7). "Abide" means *to live.* His Word lives in me to the extent that I practice it. Many Christians are born again and in Him, but His Word is not abiding in them. That's why prayer doesn't work for them.

The Word abides in me in the measure that I practice it. I may memorize it, quote it, or even preach it without it really living in me. That Word lives in me only to the measure I practice it. I let that Word have free course in me, teaching me, governing me, dominating me. I let the message of that Word take the place in my life that I would let Christ take if He were here in the flesh.

---

2 CORINTHIANS 5:17
17 Therefore if any man be IN CHRIST, he is a new creature: old things are passed away; behold, all things are become new.

Confession: "I am a new creature in Christ Jesus. I am a new creation being with the *life* of God, the *nature* of God, and the *ability* of God within me."

A Christian is not renovated like a mattress can be renovated. He is a *new creature*. He is not just made over. He is a new creation—something which never existed before. One translation reads, ". . . he is a new *species*. . . ."

The Christian at the New Birth does not have a new physical body, although he will one day. It is the man on the inside who is a new creation. The old man who used to be there is gone. The inward man is the real you (*see* 2 Cor. 4:16). And the inward man, the real man, is a new creation. He takes on the very life and nature of God.

Hold fast to your confession that you are a new creature. Then the new man on the inside will be manifested on the outside through the flesh. Learn to let this new man on the inside dominate the outward man.

God is looking at that new man in Christ when He looks at us. And we look much better *in* Christ than we do *out of* Him! We can't see each other in Christ. We look at each other from the natural standpoint, but God looks at us *in Him!*

EPHESIANS 2:10

10 For we are his workmanship, created IN CHRIST JESUS. . . .

Confession: "I am His workmanship. He made me a new creation."

We didn't make ourselves new creatures—*He* did. We are His workmanship. And you'd better be careful about how you talk about His workmanship. Be careful to say the same thing about His workmanship that He says about it in His Word. Be careful not to slur or mock God by saying, "Oh, I'm so poor and weak and unworthy. I'll never amount to anything." He didn't make you that kind of new creature. He made you a worthy new creature. He made you a new creature who could stand in His Presence as though you had never committed a sin. He made you a righteous new creature. Start telling who you actually are, instead of who you think you are.

---

2 CORINTHIANS 5:21
21 For he hath made him to be sin for us, who knew no sin; that we might be made the righteousness of God IN HIM.

Confession: "I am the righteousness of God in Christ. My standing with God is secure. My prayers avail much." (*See* James 5:16.)

We fearlessly declare that God has made us righteous. We didn't do it; *God* did it. "Righteousness" means *right-standing with God.* Jesus, who is righteous, became our righteousness. Therefore we can stand in the Presence of God as though we had never done wrong. We can stand in God's Presence without a sense of condemnation or a spiritual inferiority complex.

ROMANS 8:1
1 There is therefore now no condemnation to them which are IN CHRIST JESUS. . . .

Confession: "Because I am in Christ Jesus, *right now*—present tense—there is no sense of condemnation about me."

---

1 CORINTHIANS 1:30
30 But of him are ye IN CHRIST JESUS, who of God is made unto us wisdom, and righteousness, and sanctification, and redemption.

Confession: "Christ Jesus, my Lord, is my wisdom. He is my righteousness. He is my sanctification. He is my redemption."

ROMANS 5:17
17 For if by one man's offence death reigned by one; much more they which receive abundance of grace and of the gift of righteousness shall reign in life BY ONE, JESUS CHRIST.

Confession: "I have received abundance of grace and the gift of righteousness. I reign as a king in my domain in this life through Jesus Christ."

The *Amplified Bible* reads here, ". . . reign as kings in life through the one Man Jesus Christ. . . ." Where are we going to reign as kings? In life. In this life. How? By Jesus Christ. Paul used this illustration because they had kings in the day in which he lived. In those days the king reigned over his particular domain. His word was the final authority. Whatever he said went. He reigned. And the Word says that we shall reign in life by Christ Jesus.

In Him, We Have Redemption

COLOSSIANS 1:13–14
13 Who hath delivered us from the power of darkness, and hath translated us into the kingdom of his dear Son:
14 IN WHOM we have redemption through his blood, even the forgiveness of sins.

EPHESIANS 1:7
7 IN WHOM we have redemption through his blood, the forgiveness of sins, according to the riches of his grace.

"In whom we have redemption. . . ." How thankful we can be that we do not have to try to obtain it. We already *have* it! We are now delivered from the authority of darkness—from the power of Satan. By virtue of the New Birth, we have been delivered out of the kingdom of darkness and translated into the Kingdom of His dear Son. We can overcome the devil no matter where we meet him or what the test. Satan's dominion ended, and Jesus' dominion began in our lives the moment we accepted Jesus as Lord and were born again.

Galatians 3:13 tells us that, *"Christ hath redeemed us from the curse of the law, being made a curse for us: for it is written, Cursed is every one that hangeth on a tree."* We are redeemed from the curse of the Law! What is the curse of the Law? Go back to the first five Books of the Bible and see, especially the last half of Deuteronomy 28. In Christ, we are redeemed from the curse of the Law, which is threefold: poverty, sickness, and the Second Death. In Christ, the blessings of Abraham are ours! (*See* Galatians 3:14 and the first half of Deuteronomy 28.) Satan's dominion over us as new creatures in Christ is ended. Jesus is our Lord!

114

1 PETER 2:24
24 Who his own self bare our sins in his own body on the tree, that we, being dead to sins, should live unto righteousness: BY WHOSE stripes ye were healed.

MATTHEW 8:17
17 . . . HIMSELF took our infirmities, and bare our sicknesses.

Confession: "By His stripes I was healed! God's Word tells me that I was healed by His stripes almost two thousand years ago. If I was healed, then I am healed. Healing belongs to me, because I am *in Christ.*"

Peter, looking back to the sacrifice at Calvary said, "*. . . by whose stripes ye WERE healed*" (1 Peter 2:24). It doesn't say "*going to be*" but "*were.*" God remembers when He laid on Jesus not only the iniquities and sins of us all, but also our sicknesses and diseases. Jesus remembers that He bore them for us. Therefore, the Holy Spirit inspired Peter to write, "*. . . by whose stripes ye were healed.*" This belongs to us because we are *in Christ.* He provided it for us.

Confess that Christ is your redemption. Confess that you are redeemed. Confess that Satan has no more dominion over you, and hold fast to that confession. You have been delivered out of the kingdom of darkness. Refuse to allow Satan to have any dominion over you. Don't accept sickness—reject it.

***

ROMANS 8:2
2 For the law of the Spirit of life IN CHRIST JESUS hath made me free from the law of sin and death.

Confession: "The law of the Spirit of life in Christ Jesus has set me free from the law of sin and death."

***

Dr. John G. Lake was a missionary to Africa many years before the modern Full Gospel movement. The deadly bubonic plague broke out in his area, and hundreds died. He cared for the sick and buried the dead. Finally the British sent a ship with supplies and a corps of doctors. The doctors sent for Lake to come aboard and asked him, "What have you been using to protect yourself against this disease?"

"Sirs," Lake replied, "I believe the law of the Spirit of life in Christ Jesus has set me free from the law of sin and death. And as long as I walk in the light of that law of life, no germ will attach itself to me."

"Don't you think you had better use our preventatives?" one doctor urged.

"No," Lake said, "but, Doctor, I think you would like to experiment with me. If you will go over to one of these dead people and take the foam that comes out of his lungs after death. I'll put it under the microscope, and you will see masses of living germs. You will find they are alive until a reasonable time after a man is dead. You can fill my hand with them and I will keep my hand under the microscope. Instead of these germs remaining alive this time, they will die instantly."

The doctors agreed. They made the experiment, and it was true. When they expressed wonder at what caused it, Lake told them, "That is the law of the Spirit of life in Christ Jesus."

JAMES 4:7
7 . . . Resist the devil, and he will flee from you.

"You" is the understood subject of this sentence. *You* resist the devil and he will flee from you. He will run from you as if in terror! God has already done all He is going to do about it. He sent Jesus, and Jesus arose victorious over the devil. Jesus defeated him for you. Now it is your turn to do something about it. And you can, because you are *in Him*. Oh, the devil's not so afraid of you as an individual. But when you find out what your rights and privileges are *in Christ*—when you find out the Name of Jesus belongs to you and learn what that Name will do—then he will run from you as in terror!

1 JOHN 4:4
4 Ye are of God, little children, and have overcome them: because greater is he that is in you, than he that is in the world.

Confession: "Because I am in Christ, the Greater One lives in me. He is Greater than the devil. Greater than disease. Greater than circumstances. And He lives in me!"

Not only are we born of God and partakers of His love, but we have dwelling within us the Spirit of Him who raised Jesus from the dead (Rom. 8:11)! You may be facing some problem which seems impossible. Instead of talking about how impossible it is, look to Him who is inside you and say, "God is in me now." Your confession of faith will cause Him to work in your behalf. He will rise up in you and give you success. The Master of Creation is in you!

ROMANS 8:37
37 Nay, in all these things we are more than conquerors THROUGH HIM that loved us.

Confession: "I am a conqueror!"

If God's Word had just told us we were conquerors, it would have been enough. But the Word tells us that we are *more* than conquerors through Him. Rather than saying, "I'm defeated," rise up and say what the Bible says about you. Say, "I am a conqueror!" It may not seem to you that you are a conqueror, but your confession of it, because of what you see in God's Word, will create the reality of it in your life. Sooner or later you will become what you confess. You will not be afraid of any circumstances. You will not be afraid of any disease. You will not be afraid of any conditions. You will face life fearlessly, a conqueror!

PHILIPPIANS 4:13
13 I can do all things THROUGH CHRIST which strengtheneth me.

Confession: "Through Christ, my Lord, I can do all things. He strengthens me. I cannot be conquered. I cannot be defeated. I can do all things through Him."

Flesh and natural human reasoning would limit us to our own ability. We look to the circumstances, the problems, and the tests and storms and say that we can't. The language of doubt, the flesh, and the senses is, "I can't. I haven't the ability, the opportunity, or the strength. I'm limited." But the language of *faith* says, "I can do all things through Christ which strengtheneth me." The strength of God is ours. We do not trust in our own strength—the Bible says nothing about our being strong in ourselves. It says that *God* is our strength.

_____

GALATIANS 2:20
20 I am crucified WITH CHRIST: nevertheless I live; yet not I, but Christ liveth in me: and the life which I now live in the flesh I live by the faith of the Son of God, who loved me, and gave himself for me.

Confession: "I am crucified with Christ. I don't have to *try* to do it. I *am* crucified with Christ. Yet, nevertheless I live! And Christ lives in me!"

_____

COLOSSIANS 1:26–27
26 Even the mystery which hath been hid from ages and from generations, but now is made manifest to his saints:

27 To whom God would make known what is the riches of the glory of this mystery among the Gentiles; which is CHRIST IN YOU, the hope of glory.

Confession: "Christ lives in me!"

EPHESIANS 2:1, 4–6
1 And you hath he quickened, who were dead in trespasses and sins. . . .
4 But God, who is rich in mercy, for his great love wherewith he loved us,
5 Even when we were dead in sins, hath quickened us together WITH CHRIST, (by grace ye are saved;)
6 And hath raised us up together, and made us sit together in heavenly places IN CHRIST JESUS.

Confession: "I was crucified with Christ. When He was quickened and made alive, I was quickened *with* Him. I was raised up together with Him and was made to sit together with Him in heavenly places. Today, positionally, I am seated with Christ in heavenly places."

PHILIPPIANS 4:19
19 But my God shall supply all your need according to his riches in glory BY CHRIST JESUS.

Confession: "All my needs are supplied!"

EPHESIANS 1:3
3 Blessed be the God and Father of our Lord Jesus Christ, who hath blessed us with all spiritual blessings in heavenly places IN CHRIST.

Notice it doesn't say He is *going* to bless us with anything but that *He already has* blessed us! This means that in Christ Jesus, from the time you are born again until you step out into eternity, He has already made provision for you. Everything you need, He has blessed you with; it is yours. In the mind of God it is yours. In His Word, find the provisions He has made for His children and make them become a reality in your life in Christ—to the glory of God the Father!

The following are scripture references that include expressions such as "in Christ," "in Him," and so forth. They tell you *who you are* or *what you are* and *what you have* because you are "in Him."

Meditate on these scriptures. Confess them out loud. Faith's confessions create realities!

In Christ

Romans 3:24	Gal. 3:26	1 Thess. 4:16
Romans 8:1–2	Gal. 3:28	1 Thess. 5:18
Romans 12:5	Gal. 5:6	1 Tim. 1:14
1 Cor. 1:2	Gal. 6:15	2 Tim. 1:9

1 Cor. 1:30	Eph. 1:3	2 Tim. 1:13
1 Cor. 15:22	Eph. 1:10	2 Tim. 2:1
2 Cor. 1:21	Eph. 2:6	2 Tim. 2:10
2 Cor. 2:14	Eph. 2:10	2 Tim. 3:15
2 Cor. 3:14	Eph. 2:13	Philem. 1:6
2 Cor. 5:17	Eph. 3:6	2 Peter 1:8
2 Cor. 5:19	Phil. 3:13–14	
Gal. 2:4	Col. 1:28	

In Him

Acts 17:28	Phil. 3:9	1 John 3:3
John 1:4	Col. 2:6–7	1 John 3:5–6
John 3:15–16	Col. 2:10	1 John 3:24
2 Cor. 1:20	1 John 2:5–6	1 John 4:13
2 Cor. 5:21	1 John 2:8	1 John 5:14–15
Eph. 1:4	1 John 2:27–28	1 John 5:20
Eph. 1:10	1 John 3:3	

In the Beloved

Eph. 1:6

In the Lord

Eph. 5:8	Eph. 6:1

In Whom

Eph. 1:7	1 Peter 1:8	Col. 1:14
Eph. 1:11	Eph. 2:21–22	Col. 2:3
Eph. 1:13	Eph. 3:12	Col. 2:11

By (Through) Christ

Romans 3:22	2 Cor. 5:18	Phil. 4:19
Romans 5:15	Gal. 2:16	1 Peter 1:3
Romans 5:17–19	Eph. 1:5	1 Peter 2:5
Romans 7:4	Phil. 1:11	1 Peter 5:10
1 Cor. 1:4		

By Him

1 Cor. 1:5	Col. 1:20	Heb. 13:15
1 Cor. 8:6	Col. 3:17	1 Peter 1:21
Col. 1:16–17	Heb. 7:25	

By Himself

Heb. 1:3	Heb. 9:26

By His Blood

Heb. 9:11–12	Heb. 10:19–20	1 John 1:7
Heb. 9:14–15		

By Whom

Romans 5:2   Romans 5:11   Gal. 6:14

From Whom

Eph. 4:16   Col. 2:19

Of Christ

2 Cor. 2:15   Col. 2:17   Col. 3:24

Phil. 3:12

Of Him

1 John 1:5   1 John 2:27

Through Christ

Romans 5:1   1 Cor. 15:57   Phil. 4:6–7

Romans 5:11   Gal. 3:13–14   Phil. 4:13

Romans 6:11   Gal. 4:7   Heb. 10:10

Romans 6:23   Eph. 2:7   Heb. 13:20–21

Through Him

John 3:17   Romans 8:37   1 John 4:9

Romans 5:9

With Christ

Romans 6:8	Eph. 2:5	Col. 3:1
Gal. 2:20	Col. 2:20	Col. 3:3

With Him

Romans 6:4	Romans 8:32	Col. 3:4
Romans 6:6	2 Cor. 13:4	2 Tim. 2:11–12
Romans 6:8	Col. 2:12–15	

By Me

John 6:57	John 14:6

In Me

John 6:56	John 15:4–5	John 16:33
John 14:20	John 15:7–8	

In My Love

John 15:9

In My Name

Matt. 18:20	John 14:13–14	1 Cor. 6:11
Mark 16:17–18	John 16:23–24	

The following verses do not use the specific phrases "in Him," "in whom," and so forth, but they convey the message of who you are, what you are, or what you have *because of Christ.* (A partial listing only.)

Matt. 8:17	Phil. 2:5	James 4:7
Matt. 11:28–30	Phil. 2:13	1 Peter 2:9
Matt. 18:11	Col. 1:13	1 Peter 2:21
Matt. 18:18–20	Col. 1:26–27	1 Peter 3:18
Matt. 28:18–20	Titus 2:14	1 Peter 5:7
Mark 1:8	Titus 3:7	Heb. 13:8
Mark 9:23	Heb. 2:9–11	1 John 1:9
Mark 11:23–24	Heb. 2:14–15	1 John 2:1
Luke 10:19	Heb. 2:18	1 John 3:2
John 4:14	Heb. 4:14–16	1 John 3:14
John 6:40	Heb. 7:19	1 John 4:4
John 10:10	Heb. 7:22	1 John 4:10
John 14:12	Heb. 8:6	1 John 4:15
John 14:23	Heb. 9:24	1 John 5:1
John 17:23	Heb. 9:28	1 John 5:4–5
Gal. 3:29	Heb. 10:14	1 John 5:11–12
Gal. 5:1	Heb. 13:5–6	Rev. 1:5–6

— Chapter 7 —
God's Word—God's Medicine

My son, attend to my words; incline thine ear unto my sayings.

Let them not depart from thine eyes; keep them in the midst of thine heart.

For they are life unto those that find them, and health to all their flesh.

—Proverbs 4:20–22

The margin of a good reference Bible renders that last phrase, ". . . and *medicine* to all their flesh." God is interested in healing us if we are sick. He is also interested in keeping us well. For our healing and health, He has made provision—*God's medicine.*

What are those provisions? What are our rights? What actually belongs to us when it comes to physical healing and health? How can we ascertain exactly what was secured for us?

There's only one way. By a *constant, careful, diligent, reverent, prayerful* study of God's Word!

129

I was born sick. I never had a normal childhood. I never ran and played like other children. I never had a good night's sleep. I never had a well day until I was seventeen years old. As a little child, and then as a teenager, I'd sit and look around "open-mouthed and bugged-eyed" at things normal children could do. The greatest, consuming desire of my heart was to be well.

At the age of fifteen, I became totally bedfast. It was on this bed of sickness where I lay sixteen months that I knew if there were any help for me, it had to be in the Bible. It had to be from God. It couldn't be from anywhere else, for medical science had turned its face away and said nothing could be done. I had to come down to the brink of the grave before I did what I'm urging you to do now—come to God's Word in a constant, careful, diligent, reverent, prayerful manner and find out what God's Word has to say on this subject of healing.

I almost waited too late. If I'd had something acute, I guess I would have been carried out into eternity. But because of my condition, although it was terminal, I lingered, and I had time to do a little studying. It wasn't just overnight that I found what God had to say on the subject. Do you know why? Sometimes we have to unlearn things before we can learn the right things. Our minds have been clouded up and filled with a lot of things which are not really so.

Every time I'd get a good promise from God's Word, the devil would be right there to tell me, "That just belongs to the Jews." Or, "That's not for people nowadays."

I didn't know if it was or not. I'd have to look a long time for a scripture which proved to my own satisfaction that it belonged to me, such as our text: *"MY SON, attend to my words; incline thine ear unto my sayings"* (Prov. 4:20). God's Word doesn't just belong to the Jews. Thank God, it belongs to all of His people. As Christians, we have become God's children, and God's Word and His blessings belong to us too.

Directions for Taking God's Medicine

Suppose you were to go to the doctor and get a prescription which says: Take two capsules, three times a day, before meals. If you expect that prescription to work for you, you'd expect that you'd have to take it according to the directions.

Did you know that God gives directions for taking *His* prescription—*His* medicine?

God prescribes His Word for our healing and health, because He says, ". . . *they* [My words] *are LIFE unto those that find them, and HEALTH* [or medicine] *to all their flesh"* (Prov. 4:22).

But medicine, even in the natural, won't do you any good unless you take it. You could go to a doctor; the doctor could prescribe medicine; and you could go home and set that medicine on the chest of drawers or on the table right at your bedside. And you could still grow steadily worse. You might call the doctor and say, "I don't understand it. I got this prescription filled. I paid money for it. But I'm getting worse."

The doctor might ask, "Are you taking it according to directions?

"Well, no. But I've got it right here in the bottle at my bedside."

It won't work just because it's in the bottle. You've got to get it *in you!*

Similarly, God's medicine won't work just because you have it on a table by your bed. God's Word won't work just because you have a Bible lying on the chest of drawers. It won't even work just because you read it. It won't work just because you memorize a few scriptures. It won't work just because you say, "I believe the Bible is so." It won't work just because you say, "I believe in the verbal inspiration of the Word of God."

But it will work if you'll get it down on the inside of you, into your heart! The way you do that is not by just reading it and forgetting it, but by meditating upon it—by thinking and feeding upon it until it becomes a part of your inward man.

God's Medicine is His Word—and here are His directions for taking it.

Number One: 'My Son, Attend to My Words'

What does God mean by, "*Attend* to My words?" If I were to see a friend downtown, I might call to him as he hurries along the street: "Wait a minute! I want to talk to you."

"Oh no, Brother Hagin," he might say, "I can't talk now. I have an appointment down the street, and I'm already ten minutes late. I must *attend* to this business."

He doesn't mean to slight me. He's not angry with me. He likes me. He'd like to talk with me and fellowship with me. But there's something else he has to put first. There's something else he must give his undivided attention to.

Dr. Lilian B. Yeomans, a medical doctor who received divine healing for herself and then devoted her life to ministering and teaching this subject, would teach what she called "healing classes" in the daytime during her revival meetings. She wrote in one of her books to this effect, "I almost become angry sometimes, for when we're studying the Word of God on such an important subject as healing for the body, you can tell people are not paying a bit of attention to it. They'll thumb through the songbook, stare off into space, look out the window, chew gum. And then those same people want you to pray the prayer of faith for them. Yet they don't want to do anything *themselves*."

God wants His children to grow spiritually, and He has provided the means whereby we can grow. The Holy Spirit, through Peter said, *"As newborn babes, desire the sincere milk of the word, that ye may grow thereby"* (1 Peter 2:2).

I believe that God wants each of His children to grow spiritually, to develop a prayer life, and to develop a faith life until he can stand on his own two feet—until he is no longer a spiritual babe who has to depend on someone else to do his praying for him, to exercise faith for him, and to get his healing for him.

I would be concerned if I didn't know more about praying and have more faith than I did forty, fifty, or sixty years ago. In this day in which we live, I would become fearful, not knowing what might happen to me. But, thank God, we can walk with God. We can walk with His Word. His Word can be more real to us today than it was last year. We can learn how to pray until our prayers can be more effective this year than they were last year. Our faith can be greater this year than it was last year. And God can be more real to us this year than He was last year. He will be if we do what He said: *"My son, attend to my words . . ."* (Prov. 4:20).

Jesus said, *". . . Man shall not live by bread alone, but by every word that proceedeth out of the mouth of God"* (Matt. 4:4).

God said, "Attend to My words." That means, "Put My words first." That means, "Give My words your undivided attention." That means, "Other things *out*—My Word *in.*"

Number Two: 'Incline Thine Ear Unto My Sayings'

"Open your ears," God said, "to My sayings." In other words, open your ears to God's Word.

Incline your ear to what? "To My sayings." Open your ears to what God has to say.

"But I just don't understand it," someone says.

God doesn't ask us to understand His Word. All He asks us to do is believe it. I don't understand how a lot of spiritual things work. But, thank God, they still work! And they work because we believe.

You couldn't give an explanation from the natural viewpoint of just how the New Birth works, could you? Or just how believing on the Lord Jesus Christ and receiving Him as your Savior and confessing Him as your Lord causes you to become born again. Or just how the Spirit bears witness with your spirit that you're a child of God. But, thank God, you know it. You may not understand how it all works, but you've believed and experienced it.

You couldn't explain the workings of just how a person is filled with the Holy Spirit and speaks with other tongues. But, thank God, it's so!

Well, I can't tell a person just how divine healing works. But I know what makes it work. It's faith! *Faith* makes it work!

That's the reason God said, "Put My Word first. Attend to My words. Incline your ear to My Word"— because ". . . *faith cometh by hearing, and hearing by the word of God*" (Rom. 10:17)!

When the Word gains entrance into your heart— into your spirit—faith will be there automatically. You won't have to seek; you won't have to search. There will be no effort on your part. Faith will come unconsciously into your spirit as you feed upon and accept His words.

And faith is the clue. It's the secret. It was the secret in the healings Jesus performed when He was upon the earth.

He said to the centurion, ". . . *Go thy way; and AS THOU HAST BELIEVED, so be it done unto thee . . .*" (Matt. 8:13). And "in the selfsame hour," the centurion's servant was healed (v. 13).

When the woman with the issue of blood touched His garment, Jesus said, *"Daughter, THY FAITH hath made thee whole; go in peace, and be whole of thy plague"* (Mark 5:34).

Jairus came on behalf of his little daughter who was lying at home at the point of death. He besought Jesus saying, ". . . *come and lay thy hands on her, that she may be healed; and she shall live"* (Mark 5:23). But as Jesus started toward his house, the woman with the issue of blood came and touched His garment and was healed. Jesus was detained. Then some people from Jairus' house came and said, "Don't trouble the Master anymore. Your daughter is dead."

What could be more hopeless? It was seemingly all over for Jairus (Mark 5:35).

But Jesus turned to him and said, ". . . *Be not afraid, ONLY BELIEVE"* (v. 36). Fear not—only believe!

Jesus made His way to that house and that little maid was raised up and healed.

137

Two blind men followed Jesus after He had gone to Jairus' house to raise up Jairus' daughter. The blind men were crying and saying, *". . . Thou Son of David, have mercy on us"* (Matt. 9:27). Jesus said, *". . . Believe ye that I am able to do this? They said unto him, Yea, Lord"* (v. 28). Then Jesus touched their eyes saying, *". . . ACCORDING TO YOUR FAITH be it unto you"* (v. 29). And their eyes were opened.

Faith is what makes divine healing work. And God has told us exactly how faith comes. In Romans 10:17 He said, *"So then faith cometh. . . ."* We know it comes. From where does it come? *How* does it come? *"So then faith cometh by HEARING. . . ."* It doesn't come by *seeing.* It doesn't come by *feeling.* It comes by *hearing.* Hearing what? *"So then faith cometh by hearing, and hearing BY THE WORD OF GOD."* It comes by hearing the Word of God!

No wonder God said, "Incline thine ear unto My sayings." That's how faith comes! That's how faith for healing comes!

Let me repeat again Proverbs 4:22: *"For they* [My words] *are life unto those that find them, and health* [or medicine] *to all their flesh."*

I never could figure out why Christians, if they got sick, wouldn't take the time to find out what God has to say or wouldn't listen to what God says about healing. Instead of opening their ears to what God has to say, they listen to what everyone else has to say.

People can be right in their hearts and wrong in their heads. I don't mean it harshly, but I learned long ago that unless people are going to give you the Word of God on a subject, you can't listen to what they say—even preachers. Good men sometimes give natural advice which would cause a person to miss it spiritually.

God said, ". . . *incline thine ear unto MY sayings*" (Prov. 4:20). If you're going to listen to God, you sometimes have to shut out other things.

We have to listen to what God says in His Word to enjoy the blessings of His Word. We have to listen to what God says along any line to enjoy the blessing God has for us. So, "incline thine ear"; listen to what God has to say. Does He have anything to say about sickness? He has much to say about sickness. The following is a sampling:

His Word says, ". . . *Himself took our infirmities, and bare our sicknesses*" (Matt. 8:17).

His Word says, "*Who his own self bare our sins in his own body on the tree, that we, being dead to sins, should live unto righteousness: by whose stripes ye were healed*" (1 Peter 2:24).

139

His Word says, *"How God anointed Jesus of Nazareth with the Holy Ghost and with power: who went about doing good, and healing all that were oppressed of the devil . . ."* (Acts 10:38). Notice God calls sickness satanic oppression.

Number Three: 'Let My Words Not Depart From Thine Eyes'

In Proverbs 4:21, God tells us to look as well as listen. What did He say to listen to? His words. What does He say to look at? *His words.*

This verse has to do with healing, because in this context, He talks about life, and health, and medicine. So, do what God said to do. Get the words on healing; get the words on health. Get God's Word and look at it. Don't let it depart from before your eyes. Don't look to anything else. Just look at that Word.

And that Word says, *". . . by whose stripes ye WERE healed"* (1 Peter 2:24). Past tense—ye *were.* Then if that Word doesn't depart from before your eyes, you're bound to see yourself well. You're bound to see yourself with what God says belongs to you—if that Word doesn't depart from before your eyes.

If you see yourself sick, unhealed, or getting worse, that Word has departed from before your eyes. You're looking at something else. You're seeing yourself with something other than what the Word says you have.

No one told me. I had no teaching on the subject. But it's amazing how the Holy Spirit, as your Teacher, will lead you in line with the Word. He's the Author of it. And I didn't realize until afterward that the Holy Spirit could lead me. I received unconscious direction. But I remember the turning point in my own case of receiving healing for my body. I was bedfast for a total of sixteen months. This happened in the month of March, the twelfth month of my being bedfast.

For the preceding eleven months, I saw myself dead. Oh, I went through it a thousand times—probably ten thousand. When you're bedfast twenty-four hours a day with nothing to do except live with your physical symptoms and trouble, you can think a lot. I saw myself getting worse. I saw myself dying. In the nighttime—when all the lights were out, when everyone was asleep and I was left alone with my thoughts—many a time, night after night, I saw myself dead.

I saw my body. I saw the undertaker come and take it to the funeral home. I saw them prepare it for burial. I saw them put it in a casket. I saw them bring it back out to the house and set it in the living room. I saw the family gather around. I heard their cries and saw their tears. I saw them go to the church. I saw them roll the casket down the aisle. I saw the preacher stand before the pulpit. I heard his sermon. I heard the songs. I saw them go around for the last time and look in the casket. I came along with them and looked at it too—it was me. I saw my face, cold and white. I saw myself dead.

I saw them roll the casket up the aisle. I saw the pallbearers put it in the hearse. I saw them come down old Highway 75 and turn off into the Forrest Grove Cemetery. I could see the newly dug grave. I saw them come down to the family burial plot. I saw them set the casket there, put flowers around it, and have a final graveside rite. I saw the friends and family leave, get in their cars, and go home. I saw the casket lowered into the box with a lid put on it. I heard the clods as they fell on the lid. I saw them fill it with dirt, mound it up, and lay the flowers on it. I saw those flowers wither and die till they were all gone. I saw that grave in that old cemetery. I saw myself dead.

I saw the leaves on the trees finally wither and die until the trees stood bare in the cold of winter. I saw the rain and snow of winter come. I saw spring come. I heard the birds sing. I saw the summertime sun beating down upon that grave. I saw myself dead.

But somewhere, there was a glimmer of hope, a beam of light from the Word, that aroused me to stand my ground and refuse to die! And I can remember, it was after I read this portion of Scripture: *"Let them not depart from thine eyes . . ."* (Prov. 4:21).

Somehow I knew it would work. I didn't understand it. I'd never heard it preached. I was just a boy of sixteen. But I knew it was God's Word. I knew He said, "My Words are medicine." I knew He said, "My Word is health to all their flesh." That meant from the top of my head to the soles of my feet! I also knew that five doctors said they couldn't do a thing—that I had to die. But I began to see myself well!

Afterward, when some of those heart attacks would come, and I'd seem to get worse, I'd laugh. I'd just laugh right in the face of them! I'd see myself well!

I asked myself the question, "What would I be doing if I were up?"

I answered, "I'd be preaching."

So I said, "Give me a pencil and paper." And I started working up some sermons. I only ever preached one of them; they were unpreachable. But eventually I had a whole box of them. I saw myself well.

Can you see what I'm talking about? Don't let His Words depart from before your eyes.

Why?

They are life! They are *life*!

Number Four: 'Keep My Words in the Midst of Your Heart'

That means in the very core of your being—in your spirit, your inner man. The Psalmist said, *"Thy word have I hid in mine heart, that I might not sin against thee"* (119:11). Later in this chapter, I'll give you an example of how to do this.

Now what are the results? (Thank God, God's Word produces results!) What are the results of following these directions and keeping God's Word in the midst of your heart? They will be life unto those who find them, and health to all their flesh!

As a Baptist boy on the bed of sickness, I wrote in red ink on the flyleaf of my Bible: "My motto—*The Bible says it. I believe it. And that settles it!"*

To me, when I read the Bible, it's God's Word. I believe it, and that settles it. And that's the end of it. There's no use in discussing it, because the Bible says so. His Words are health; they are medicine to all their flesh.

Someone asked, "Brother Hagin, are you ever sick?"

"No."

"Well, yeah," he said, "but you know what I mean." And this man was a Full Gospel preacher, a Spirit-filled preacher praying for the sick! He said, "I'll tell you what I take. I've found it helps me so much," and he gave me a long rigmarole of everything he was taking to keep him going so he could preach divine healing. Then he asked, "What do you take?"

I said, "I take what I preach. If it doesn't work for me, I don't know how in the world it would work for anyone else."

"Yes, but do you ever feel just a little 'draggy'?"

"Not often," I said.

"Well, if you do feel a little under the weather, what do you do?"

I said, "I just double up on the medicine. I just double the dose. I double up on my Bible reading, and it works wonders!"

God's Medicine: To Be Applied From the Heart

God's medicine, like all His provisions—salvation, for instance—is to be believed and applied from the heart, the spirit.

What often happens, however, is this: People read certain promises—perhaps they can even quote them—and they endeavor to act upon them without really getting them into their spirits. It's more in their heads than in their hearts.

I always do it this way. I don't pray about some things just right away. For example, years ago, I was in a meeting in Texas City, Texas. Pat, our daughter, was a little girl at the time. She had developed a growth, not a sty, but a growth of some kind near her eye. Before I left home to travel to the Texas City meeting, I had laid hands on her and prayed. But when my wife wrote me on Monday, the growth was still there.

She wrote, "Pat wants to know what to tell the nurse when she comes around to check next Monday."

Once a month, a nurse came around to the grade schools and checked their eyes and ears. Pat knew that when the nurse found that knot, she would ask if we'd taken her to a doctor. And we hadn't. So all Pat wanted to know was, "What am I going to tell the nurse?"

I received the letter on Tuesday, and I knew I had a little time before I had to answer her. I pushed it out of my mind until after the evening service so my attention wouldn't be divided.

That night after the service I returned to my hotel, listened to the news from 10:00 to 10:15, turned off the radio, and at 10:15, I picked up my Bible and said to myself, *I'm going to read the Bible for an hour on the subject of healing.*

I daresay I could have quoted ninety percent of all the verses in the Bible on the subject of healing. They were all marked in my Bible. But I started with the Book of Genesis and read these verses, very slowly, right on down through the New Testament.

At 11:15, I closed my Bible, turned off the light, and said, *I'm going to lie here an hour and meditate on these scriptures.*

One well-known teacher of the Word has pointed out that one meaning of the word "meditate" in the Old Testament is *to mutter.* That's what I did. There in the nighttime in bed, I muttered those scriptures to myself.

At 12:15 I said to myself, *I'm going to sleep for an hour. Then I'm going to wake up and meditate on these scriptures for an hour. Then I'll sleep an hour and wake up and meditate an hour until morning.*

And I did that. The Holy Spirit dwells in your spirit. Your body needs rest and sleep, but really your spirit doesn't. I have an alarm on the inside of me. I just said to my spirit, *I'm going to sleep an hour,* and in an hour my spirit awakened me. Then

I would meditate on these scriptures on healing for an hour.

What I needed right then was healing for my daughter. There was no use in my meditating on anything else. There was no need in my thinking about scriptures that promise finances. That's not what I needed right then.

I did that right on through the night. And the next night I did the same thing. After the news, I picked up my Bible and slowly read through the scriptures on divine healing, meditated an hour, slept an hour, meditated an hour, slept an hour, right on through the second night.

Then on Thursday afternoon, I wrote my wife. I said, "In the letter you wrote me Monday, you said Pat wanted to know what to tell the nurse."

(I didn't tell her what to tell the nurse. You see, I had taken the Word of God and built it into my spirit. And I didn't go by what I knew about it in my head.)

I wrote, "You tell Pat that Daddy said she's healed. And I know in my heart that she's healed, just as well as I know in my head that two plus two is four, and three times three is nine." And that's all I wrote about it.

(You've got to know God's Word in your spirit—that's *real* faith—just like you know other things in your head, such as principles of addition and multiplication.)

My wife told me later that she got the letter, read it, and then put it aside till Pat came in from school. Pat was outside playing with her dolls when my wife remembered the letter and called her inside.

"Pat, we got a letter from Daddy, and here's what he said: 'You tell Pat that Daddy said she's healed. And I know it in my heart that she's healed, just as well as I know in my head that two plus two is four, and three times three is nine.'"

My wife said Pat stood there a minute as if she were thinking about it. Then she said, "If Daddy says so, it's so." She turned around and skipped outside again to play.

By Monday, the growth had disappeared. It was gone. She didn't have to tell the nurse anything. And I never did answer that question.

Get the Word of God—God's medicine—built into your spirit.

A wife may know about cooking. She may be able to sit down to a table with nothing on it and explain to her husband all about a delicious recipe, every ingredient in it, and just how to prepare it. But just because she knows all that won't put anything into his stomach. Just knowing that won't put anything in her stomach either.

You have to cook up the dish you know how to fix, and then you have to eat it. Even prepared and sitting on the table, your talking about it won't do anything for you.

That's how it is with the Bible. It's right there— and we talk about it. We discuss the Scriptures and quote them. But they really don't get in us. The Word doesn't get down into our spirits like it should. That's why it doesn't work for us.

To keep your faith strong, keep feeding it. Constantly feed along faith lines. I often tell folks that just because I ate a T-bone steak once doesn't mean I'm going to say, "I know how that tastes. I've had one, so I'm never going to eat another one." No. I'll eat one every chance I get! Continual feeding and exercise of the body keeps it strong. Similarly, continually feeding and exercising the spirit keeps it strong.

I took something from P.C. Nelson many, many years ago. He said, "Constantly feed along the line of faith and healing. Do it constantly with whatever else you read."

Every day, as a usual thing, no matter what else I'm reading, I'll read something along the line of faith and healing. I constantly feed along this line.

Now someone might say, "I'm just going to believe it will work. It worked for Kenneth Hagin, so it will work for me."

But if they don't do the same thing I did, it won't work for them. Because *their* faith is not being fed. Jesus said, "According to *your* faith, be it unto you" (Matt. 9:29).

As "Dad" Nelson said, "The time will come that you will need faith, either for yourself or for some member of your family. And if you haven't kept your faith strong, you'll be at a disadvantage."

Get the Word of God—God's medicine—built into your spirit!

Medication for Meditation— Healing in the Atonement

ISAIAH 53:4–5
4 Surely he [Jesus] **hath borne our griefs** [or sicknesses]**, and carried our sorrows** [or pains]**: yet we did esteem him stricken, smitten of God, and afflicted.**
5 But he was wounded for our transgressions, he was bruised for our iniquities: the chastisement of our peace was upon him; and with his stripes we are healed.

MATTHEW 8:16–17
16 . . . and [Jesus] **healed all that were sick:**

17 That it might be fulfilled which was spoken by Esaias [Isaiah] the prophet, saying, Himself took our infirmities, and bare our sicknesses.

1 PETER 2:24
24 Who his own self bare our sins in his own body on the tree, that we, being dead to sins, should live unto righteousness: by whose stripes ye were healed.

GALATIANS 3:13
13 Christ hath redeemed us from the curse of the law, being made a curse for us: for it is written, Cursed is every one that hangeth on a tree.

According to Deuteronomy 28:15–22, 27–29, 35–61, *all* sickness and disease is a curse of the Law. But, praise God, according to Galatians 3:13, Christ has redeemed us from the curse of the Law!

Healing, the Will of the Father

EXODUS 15:26
26 . . . for I am the LORD that healeth thee.

EXODUS 23:25–26
25 And ye shall serve the Lord your God, and he shall bless thy bread, and thy water; and I will take sickness away from the midst of thee.
26 There shall nothing cast their young, nor be barren, in thy land: the number of thy days I will fulfil.

2 CHRONICLES 16:9

9 For the eyes of the Lord run to and fro throughout the whole earth, to shew himself strong in the behalf of them whose heart is perfect toward him. . . .

PSALM 91:10, 16

10 There shall no evil befall thee, neither shall any plague come nigh thy dwelling. . . .

16 With long life will I satisfy him, and shew him my salvation.

PSALM 103:2–3

2 Bless the Lord, O my soul, and forget not all his benefits:

3 Who forgiveth all thine iniquities; who healeth all thy diseases.

PSALM 107:20

20 He sent his word, and healed them. . . .

ISAIAH 55:11

11 So shall my word be that goeth forth out of my mouth: it shall not return unto me void, but it shall accomplish that which I please, and it shall prosper in the thing whereto I sent it.

MATTHEW 7:11

11 If ye then, being evil [natural], know how to give good gifts unto your children, how much more shall your Father which is in heaven give good things to them that ask him?

JAMES 1:17

17 Every good gift and every perfect gift is from above, and cometh down from the Father of lights. . . .

153

MATTHEW 8:2-3
2 And, behold, there came a leper and worshipped him, saying, Lord, if thou wilt, thou canst make me clean.
3 And Jesus put forth his hand, and touched him, saying, I will; be thou clean. . . .

Jesus said of Himself, *"For I came . . . not to do mine own will, but the will of him that sent me"* (John 6:38). Everything Jesus did in His earth walk was the will of the Father. He was the will of God in action. If you want to know the will of the Father, look at Jesus.

Healing: The Works of Jesus

ACTS 10:38
38 How God anointed Jesus of Nazareth with the Holy Ghost and with power: who went about doing good, and healing all that were oppressed of the devil. . . .

A fact to settle in your heart: *Christ is the Healer; Satan is the oppressor.*

JOHN 10:10
10 The thief cometh not, but for to steal, and to kill, and to destroy: I am come that they might have life, and that they might have it more abundantly.

MATTHEW 9:35
35 And Jesus went about all the cities and villages, teaching in their synagogues, and preaching the gospel of the kingdom, and healing every sickness and every disease among the people.

MATTHEW 15:30–31
30 And great multitudes came unto him, having with them those that were lame, blind, dumb, maimed, and many others, and cast them down at Jesus' feet; and he healed them:
31 Insomuch that the multitude wondered, when they saw the dumb to speak, the maimed to be whole, the lame to walk, and the blind to see: and they glorified the God of Israel.

HEBREWS 13:8
8 Jesus Christ the same yesterday, and to day, and for ever.

JOHN 14:12
12 Verily, verily, I say unto you, He that believeth on me, the works that I do shall he do also; and greater works than these shall he do; because I go unto my Father.

MARK 16:15, 17–18
15 And he said unto them, Go ye into all the world, and preach the gospel to every creature. . . .
17 And these signs shall follow them that believe; In my name shall they cast out devils. . . .
18 . . . they shall lay hands on the sick, and they shall recover.

JAMES 5:14–15

14 Is any sick among you? let him call for the elders of the church; and let them pray over him, anointing him with oil in the name of the Lord:

15 And the prayer of faith shall save the sick, and the Lord shall raise him up; and if he have committed sins, they shall be forgiven him.

3 JOHN 2

2 Beloved, I wish above all things that thou mayest prosper and be in health, even as thy soul prospereth.

Healing: God at Work Within

1 JOHN 4:4

4 Ye are of God, little children, and have overcome them: because greater is he that is in you, than he that is in the world.

Faith for Healing/The Prayer of Faith

MARK 11:23–24

23 For verily I say unto you, That whosoever shall say unto this mountain, Be thou removed, and be thou cast into the sea; and shall not doubt in his heart, but shall believe that those things which he saith shall come to pass; he shall have whatsoever he saith.

24 Therefore I say unto you, What things soever ye desire, when ye pray, believe that ye receive them, and ye shall have them.

Why should you consider attending
Rhema
Bible Training College?

Here are a few good reasons:

- Training at one of the top Spirit-filled Bible schools anywhere
- Teaching based on steadfast faith in God's Word
- Growth in your spiritual walk coupled with practical training in effective ministry
- Specialization in the area of your choosing: Youth or Children's Ministry, Evangelism, Pastoral Care, Missions, Biblical Studies, or Supportive Ministry
- Optional intensive third- and fourth-year programs: School of Worship, School of Pastoral Ministry, School of World Missions, School of Biblical Studies, and General Extended Studies
- Worldwide ministry opportunities—while you're in school
- An established network of churches and ministries around the world who depend on Rhema to supply full-time staff and support ministers

Call today or go online for more information or application material.
1-888-28-FAITH (1-888-283-2484)
www.rbtc.org

Rhema Bible Training College admits students of any race, color, or ethnic origin.

OFFER CODE—BKORD:PRMDRBTC

Always on.

For the latest news and information on products, media, podcasts, study resources, and special offers, visit us online 24 hours a day.

Free Subscription!

Call now to receive a free subscription to *The Word of Faith* magazine from Kenneth Hagin Ministries. Receive encouragement and spiritual refreshment from . . .

- *Faith-building articles from Kenneth W. Hagin, Lynette Hagin, Craig W. Hagin, and others*

- *"Timeless Teaching" from the archives of Kenneth E. Hagin*

- *Feature articles on prayer and healing*

- *Testimonies of salvation, healing, and deliverance*

- *Children's activity page*

- *Updates on Rhema Bible Training College, Rhema Bible Church, and other outreaches of Kenneth Hagin Ministries*

Subscribe today for your free *Word of Faith*!

1-888-28-FAITH (1-888-283-2484)

www.rhema.org/wof

OFFER CODE—BKORD:WF

Rhema
Correspondence Bible School

The Rhema Correspondence Bible School is a home Bible study course that can help you in your everyday life!

This course of study has been designed with you in mind, providing practical teaching on prayer, faith, healing, Spirit-led living, and much more to help you live a victorious Christian life!

Flexible
Enroll any time: choose your topic of study; study at your own pace!

Affordable
Pay as you go—only $25 per lesson!
(Price subject to change without notice.)

Profitable

"The Lord has blessed me through a Rhema Correspondence Bible School graduate. . . . He witnessed to me 15 years ago, and the Lord delivered me from drugs and alcohol. I was living on the streets and then in somebody's tool shed. Now I lead a victorious and blessed life! I now am a graduate of Rhema Correspondence Bible School too! I own a beautiful home. I have a beautiful wife and two children who also love the Lord. The Lord allows me to preach whenever my pastor is out of town. I am on the board of directors at my church and at the Christian school. Thank you, and God bless you and your ministry!"

—D.J., Lusby, Maryland

"Thank you for continually offering Rhema Correspondence Bible School. The eyes of my understanding have been enlightened greatly through the Word of God through having been enrolled in RCBS. My life has forever been changed."

—M.R., Princeton, N.C.

For enrollment information and a course listing, call today!

1-888-28-FAITH (1-888-283-2484)

www.rhema.org/rcbs

OFFER CODE—BKORD:BRCSC